10666354

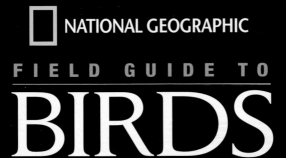

NATIONAL GEOGRAPHIC

FIELD GUIDE TO

BIRDS

NEW JERSEY

NATIONAL GEOGRAPHIC

FIELD GUIDE TO

BIRDS

Edited by JONATHAN ALDERFER

National Geographic
Washington, D.C.

INTRODUCTION

When people think of New Jersey they think of a small state (about 170 miles long by 60 miles wide) with a dense population (at more than 8 million people, it is the densest). Two of North America's largest urban centers (New York City and Philadelphia) press at its borders. Or people may remember a drive along the New Jersey Turnpike, past power plants, aging factories, and petrochemical facilities. The title "The Crossroads of Migration" probably is not the first one that comes to mind. Yet, despite its size and crush of humanity, New Jersey supports an excellent diversity of birdlife. This bounty is the result of the state's strategic coastal location and a surprising—though dwindling—amount of open space, with many of the best birding sites protected by private organizations as well as state and federal government.

Many northern and southern bird species are at or near their range limits in New Jersey. A wealth of natural habitats supports a rich diversity of birdlife. In the northwest, Appalachian ridges are breeding grounds for forest birds and funnels for migrant raptors. A variety of waterbirds inhabit wetlands such as Kearny Marsh and the Great Swamp; while woodlands including those at Palmyra and Garret Mountain support scores of migrating warblers. Staggering numbers of migrant shorebirds and nesting colonial waterbirds flock to the salt marshes and mudflats along the Atlantic coast and Delaware Bay. Coastal bays and estuaries fill with wintering and migrant waterfowl, gulls, and terns. Finally, coastal migrant traps at Sandy Hook, Island Beach State Park, and Cape May—a world-renowned birding site—attract many thousands of migrants: seabirds, hawks, flycatchers, vireos, swallows, thrushes, warblers, sparrows, and finches. New Jersey is indeed "The Crossroads of Migration."

PAUL LEHMAN
CAPE MAY, NEW JERSEY

CONTENTS

LOOKING AT BIRDS

W hat do the artist and the nature lover share? A passion for being attuned to the world and all of its complexity, via the senses. Every time you go out into the natural world, or even view it through a window, you have another opportunity to see what is there. And the more you know what you are looking at, the more you see.

Even if you are not yet a committed birder, it makes sense to take a field guide with you when you go out for a walk or a hike. Looking for and identifying birds will sharpen and heighten your perceptions, and intensify your experience. And you'll find that you notice everything else more acutely—the terrain, the season, the weather, the plant life, other animal life.

Birds are beautiful, complex animals that live everywhere around us in our towns and cities, and in distant places we dream of visiting. Here in North America more than 900 species have been recorded—from abundant commoners to the rare and exotic. A comprehensive field reference like the *National Geographic Field Guide to the Birds of North America* is essential for understanding that big picture. If you are taking a spring walk in the New Jersey countryside, however, you may want something simpler: a guide to the birds you are most likely to see, which slips easily into a pocket.

This photographic guide is designed to provide an introduction to the common birds—and a few rare birds—you might encounter in New Jersey: how to identify them, how they behave, and where to find them, with specific locations.

Discovery, observation, and identification of birds can be exciting, whether you are a novice or expert. As an artist and birder for most of my life, I know that every time I go out to look at birds, I see more clearly and have a greater appreciation for the natural world around me and my own place in it.

JONATHAN ALDERFER
Editor

*N*ational Geographic Field Guide to Birds: New Jersey* is designed to help birders at any level quickly identify birds in the field. The book is organized by bird families, following the order in the *Check-list to the Birds of North America,* by the American Ornithologists' Union. Families share structural characteristics, and by learning these shared characteristics early, birders will establish a basis for a lifetime of identifying birds and related family members with great accuracy—sometimes merely at a glance. (For quick reference in the field, use the color and alphabetical indexes at the back of this book.)

A family may have one member or dozens of members, or species. In this book each family is identified by its common name in English along the right-hand border of each spread. Each species is also identified in English, with its Latin genus and species—its scientific name—found directly underneath. One species is featured in each entry.

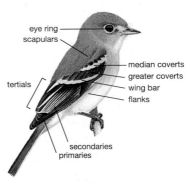

eye ring
scapulars
median coverts
greater coverts
wing bar
flanks
tertials
secondaries
primaries

Least Flycatcher

supercilium

postocular stripe

ear patch
(auricular)

moustachial stripe

submoustachial
stripe

median crown stripe

lateral crown stripe

supraloral area

lores

malar stripe

Lark Sparrow

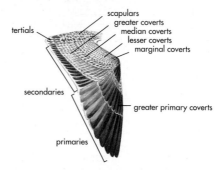

scapulars
greater coverts
median coverts
lesser coverts
marginal coverts

tertials

secondaries

greater primary coverts

primaries

Great Black-backed Gull, upper wing

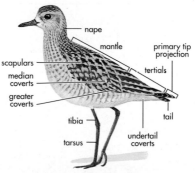

nape

mantle

scapulars

median
coverts

greater
coverts

tibia

tarsus

primary tip
projection

tertials

tail

undertail
coverts

Pacific Golden-Plover

An entry begins with **Field Marks**, the physical clues used to quickly identify a bird, such as body shape and size, bill length, and plumage color or pattern. A bird's body parts yield vital clues to identification, so a birder needs to become familiar with them early on. After the first glance at body type, take note of the head shape and markings, such as stripes, eye rings, and crown markings. Bill shape and color are important as well. Note body and wing details: wing bars, color of primary flight feathers, wing color at rest, and shape and markings when extended in flight. Tail shape, length, color, and banding may play a big part, too. At left are diagrams detailing the various parts of a bird—its topography—labeled with the term likely to be found in the text of this book.

The main body of each entry is divided into three categories: Behavior, Habitat, and Local Sites. The **Behavior** section details certain characteristics to look or listen for in the field. Often a bird's behavioral characteristics are very closely related to its body type and field marks, such as in the case of woodpeckers, whose chisel-shaped bills, stiff tails, strong legs, and sharp claws enable them to spend most of their lives in an upright position, braced against a tree trunk. The **Habitat** section describes areas that are most likely to support the featured species. Preferred nesting locations of breeding birds are also included in many cases. The **Local Sites** section recommends specific refuges or parks where the featured bird is likely to be found. A section called **Field Notes** finishes each entry, and includes information such as plumage variations within a species; or it may introduce another species with which the featured bird is frequently confused. In the latter case, an additional drawing may be included to help in identification.

Finally, a caption underneath each of the photographs explains the season of the plumage pictured, as well as the age and gender of the bird above. A key to using this informative guide and its range maps follows on the next two pages.

READING THE SPREAD

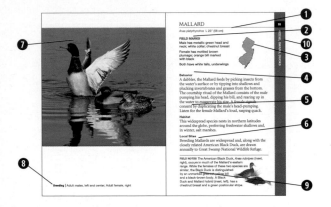

MALLARD

Anas platyrhynchos L 23" (58 cm)

FIELD MARKS

Male has metallic green head and neck; white collar; chestnut breast

Female has mottled brown plumage; orange bill marked with black

Both have white tails, underwings

Behavior

A dabbler, the Mallard feeds by picking insects from the water's surface or by tipping into shallows and plucking invertebrates and grasses from the bottom. The courtship ritual of the Mallard consists of the male pumping his head, dipping his bill, and rearing up in the water to exaggerate his size. A female signals consent by duplicating the male's head-pumping. Listen for the female Mallard's loud, rasping quack.

Habitat

This widespread species nests in northern latitudes around the globe, preferring freshwater shallows and, in winter, salt marshes.

Local Sites

Breeding Mallards are widespread and, along with the closely related American Black Duck, are drawn annually to Great Swamp National Wildlife Refuge.

FIELD NOTES The American Black Duck, *Anas rubripes* (inset, right), occurs in much of the Mallard's eastern range. While the females of these two species are similar, the Black Duck is distinguished by an unmarked greenish-yellow bill and a black-brown body. A Black Duck and Mallard hybrid (inset, left), has a chestnut breast and a green postocular stripe.

Breeding | Adult males, left and center; Adult female, right

❶ Heading: Beneath the Common Name find the Latin, or Scientific, Name. Beside it is the bird's length, and frequently wingspan. Wingspan occurs with birds often seen in flight. Female measurements are given if disparate from the male's.

❷ Field Marks: Gives basic field identification for body size, head and bill shape, and markings.

❸ Range Map: Shows year-round range in purple, breeding range in red, winter range in blue. Areas through which species are likely to migrate are shown in green.

❹ Behavior: A step beyond **Field Marks,** gives clues to identifying a bird's habits, such as feeding, flight pattern, courtship, nest-building, and songs and calls.

❺ Habitat: Reveals the area a species most likely inhabits, such as forested regions, marshy areas, cities, or farms. May include preferred nesting sites.

❻ Local Sites: Details local spots to look for a given species.

❼ Photograph: Shows bird in its habitat. May be a female or male, adult or juvenile. Plumage is breeding, molting, or nonbreeding.

❽ Caption: Defines the featured bird's plumage, age, and gender, as seen in the picture.

❾ Field Note: A special entry that may give a unique point of identification, compare two species of the same family, compare two species from different families that are easily confused, or focus on a historic or conservation fact.

❿ Band: Gives the common name of the bird's family.

On each map of New Jersey, range boundaries are drawn where the species ceases to be regularly seen. Nearly every species will be rare at the edges of its range. The sample map shown below explains the colors and symbols used on each map. Ranges continually expand and contract, so the map is a tool, not a rule. Range information is based on actual sightings and therefore depends upon the number of knowledgeable and active birders in each area.

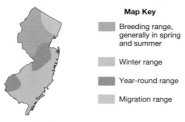

Map Key

Breeding range, generally in spring and summer

Winter range

Year-round range

Migration range

Sample Map: Savannah Sparrow

READING THE INDEXES

There are two indexes at the back of the book. The first (pg. 260) is a **Color Index**, created for birders to make quick IDs in the field. In this index, birds are labeled by their predominant color: Mostly White, Mostly Black, etc. Note that a bird may have a head of a different color than its label states. That's because its body— the part most noticeable in the field—is the color labeled.

The **Alphabetical Index** (pg. 264) is by the bird's common name. Next to each entry is a check-off box. Most birders make lists of the birds they see. Some keep several lists, perhaps one of birds in a certain area and another of all the birds they've ever seen—a life list. Such lists enable birders to look back and remember their first sighting of an Indigo Bunting or a Downy Woodpecker.

Year-round | Adult white morph

SNOW GOOSE

Chen caerulescens L 35" (89 cm) W 45" (114 cm)

FIELD MARKS
White overall

Black primaries

Pinkish bill with black "grinning patch"

Rusty stains often visible on face in summer

Behavior
Travels in huge flocks, especially during fall migration from high Arctic breeding grounds. Loud, vocal birds, sounding like baying hounds, they fly in loose V's and long lines, sometimes more than 1,500 miles nonstop, reaching speeds up to 40 mph. Agile swimmers, they commonly rest on water during migration and at wintering grounds. Listen for their harsh *wouk*.

Habitat
Most often seen on grasslands, grainfields, and coastal wetlands, favoring standing shallow freshwater marshes and flooded fields. Primarily vegetarian, this goose forages on agricultural grains and plants and on all parts of aquatic vegetation.

Local Sites
A good place to spot Snow Geese is in the Brigantine Refuge, where large flocks congregate during the day to drink fresh water before heading back to the bay to rest at night. Also try the farm fields of Salem and Cumberland Counties.

FIELD NOTES Amid a flock of white Snow Geese, you may see a few blue morphs (inset), characterized by a varying amount of dark gray-brown on the back and breast.

Year-round | Adult

BRANT

Branta bernicla L 25" (64 cm)

FIELD MARKS
Small, dark, and stocky with black
head, neck, breast, and bill

Distinctive whitish patch on each
side of neck

White uppertail coverts and black
tail conspicuous in flight

Behavior
Flocks fly low in ragged formations with no evident
lead bird. The Brant rests near open water and waits for
a falling tide to trigger its appetite. Though some
populations have adapted to wintering on grassy fields,
the birds continue to forage during low tide in nearby
bays, and lift off the fields as the tide begins to rise. Call
is a low, rolling, throaty *raunk-raunk.*

Habitat
The Brant winters along sea coasts, feeding on the
aquatic plants of shallow bays and estuaries. It breeds
on Arctic tundra, and tends to build its nest of grass
and other materials on small islands one to five miles
from the coast.

Local Sites
Look for Brants wintering in large coastal bays from
Raritan Bay south to Cape May, feeding on marine
algae in the shallow waters off the coast.

FIELD NOTES This species experienced a great decline in number
in the 1930s due to a scarcity of eelgrass, its favored food at the
time. Brants adapted to other aquatic vegetation and winter
grainfields to survive, and the species has rebounded.

Year-round | Adult

CANADA GOOSE

Branta canadensis L 30-43" (75-108 cm) W 59-73" (148-183 cm)

FIELD MARKS
Black head and neck marked with
distinctive white chin strap

In flight, shows large, dark wings,
white undertail coverts, white
U-shaped rump band

Variable pale breast color

Behavior
A common, familiar goose; best known for migrating
in large V-formation. Its distinctive musical call of
honk-a-lonk makes it easy to identify, even without
seeing it. It also makes a murmuring sound when
feeding, and a hissing sound when protecting nests or
young. The Canada Goose finds a mate when two years
old and remains monogamous for life.

Habitat
Prefers wetlands, grasslands, and cultivated fields within commuting distance of water. Breeds in open or
forested areas near water. It has adapted successfully
to man-made habitats such as golf courses and farms,
to the extent that it sometimes chases off other
nesting waterbirds.

Local Sites
Find Canada Geese in Johnson Park, on the Raritan
River in New Brunswick, or on the
ponds of corporate parks throughout
the state.

FIELD NOTES Ongoing research into the
mitochondrial DNA of the Canada
Goose has found that the smaller subspecies, such as *hutchinsii*
(inset, left) and *minima* (inset, right), actually belong to their own
species, the newly named Cackling Goose, *Branta hutchinsii*.

Year-round | Adults

TUNDRA SWAN

Cygnus columbianus L 52" (132 cm)

FIELD MARKS
White overall with black facial skin

Black, slightly concave bill with yellow spot of variable size in front of eye

Juvenile appears darker with pinkish bill

Behavior
Feeds on submerged aquatic vegetation in shallow water, using its long neck, which enables it to keep its body upright. To take flight, the Tundra Swan runs across water beating its wings. Migrates thousands of miles between Arctic breeding grounds and temperate wintering quarters, at altitudes up to 27,000 feet. Also an exceptionally fast swimmer. Call is a noisy, high-pitched whooping.

Habitat
Winters in flocks along Pacific and Atlantic coasts on shallow ponds, lakes, and estuaries. Breeds on coastal tundra of Alaska and Arctic Canada, where it nests near ponds or sheltered marshes.

Local Sites
Find wintering Tundra Swans along with many other wading birds and waterfowl in the Brigantine Division of the Edwin B. Forsythe National Wildlife Refuge.

FIELD NOTES The Mute Swan, *Cygnus olor* (inset: juvenile, left; adult, right), is identified by a black knob at the base of an orange bill. At rest, the Mute Swan holds its neck in an S-curve, its bill pointed down; the Tundra Swan's neck sticks straight up from its breast. Mute Swans are widespread year-round residents in New Jersey and can be found in the Brigantine Refuge.

Breeding | Adult male

WOOD DUCK

Aix sponsa L 18½" (47 cm)

FIELD MARKS
Glossy, colorful plumage; reddish eye in male

Short crest; large white teardrop-shaped eye patch in female

Juvenile resembles female but is spotted below

Behavior
Most commonly feeds by picking insects from the water's surface or by tipping into shallows to pluck invertebrates from the bottom, but may also be seen foraging on land. The omnivorous Wood Duck's diet changes throughout the year depending upon available foods and its need for particular proteins or minerals during migration, breeding, and molting. Male Wood Ducks give a soft, upslurred whistle when swimming. Female Wood Ducks have a distinctive rising, squealing flight call of *oo-eek*.

Habitat
Prefers woodlands and forested swamps and can be seen year-round throughout much of New Jersey. Nests in tree cavities or man-made nest boxes.

Local Sites
Great Swamp National Wildlife Refuge, east of Basking Ridge, is home to a large population of nesting Wood Ducks. Look for them in summer months in nest boxes mounted on short poles throughout the park.

FIELD NOTES Wood Duck hens are known to hatch up to eight eggs in nest holes high up in tree cavities. Once hatched, the young must make a long jump to the ground, sometimes 30 feet below. Protected by their downy newborn plumage, they generally bounce safely.

Breeding | Adult males, left and center; Adult female, right

MALLARD

Anas platyrhynchos L 23" (58 cm)

FIELD MARKS

Male has metallic green head and
neck; white collar; chestnut breast

Female has mottled brown
plumage; orange bill marked
with black

Both have white tails, underwings

Behavior
A dabbler, the Mallard feeds by picking insects from
the water's surface or by tipping into shallows and
plucking invertebrates and grasses from the bottom.
The courtship ritual of the Mallard consists of the male
pumping his head, dipping his bill, and rearing up in
the water to exaggerate his size. A female signals
consent by duplicating the male's head-pumping.
Listen for the female Mallard's loud, rasping quack.

Habitat
This widespread species nests in northern latitudes
around the globe, preferring freshwater shallows and,
in winter, salt marshes.

Local Sites
Breeding Mallards are widespread and, along with the
closely related American Black Duck, are drawn
annually to Great Swamp National Wildlife Refuge.

FIELD NOTES The American Black Duck, *Anas rubripes* (inset,
right), occurs in much of the Mallard's eastern
range. While the females of these two species are
similar, the Black Duck is distinguished by an
unmarked greenish yellow bill and a
black-brown body. A Black Duck and
Mallard hybrid (inset, left), has a
chestnut breast and a green postocular stripe.

Breeding | Adult male

NORTHERN PINTAIL

Anas acuta Male L 26" (66 cm) Female L 20" (51 cm)

FIELD MARKS
Chocolate brown head, hind neck

Long white neck, breast, and underparts; thin white line behind face extending under neck

Long black central tail feathers

Female mottled brown overall

Behavior
Often seen in small flocks during winter months foraging in flooded agricultural fields or shallow ponds and marshes. Also eats aquatic insects, snails, beetles, and small crustaceans. This elegant duck is an accomplished flyer known for spilling out of the sky in spectacular rapid descents, leveling out directly into a landing on wings which produce an audible *swish.* Male's call is a weak, nasal *geee;* female often utters a gutteral quack.

Habitat
Frequents both freshwater and saltwater marshes, ponds, lakes, and coastal bays. Also found in flooded agricultural fields, especially during winter.

Local Sites
Look for the Pintail foraging with other common waterfowl at Brigantine Refuge and at ponds in Cape May, at the southern end of the Garden State Parkway.

FIELD NOTES The Northern Pintail hen engages in an elaborate in-flight courtship ritual in which the hen veers, swerves, makes abrupt turns, and climbs, challenging her suitor to match her moves. If he succeeds, she rewards the drake by allowing him to take her tail in his beak, or to pass below her so closely that their wing tips touch. If he fails her test, the hen signals to another drake to give it a try.

Breeding | Adult male

GREEN-WINGED TEAL

Anas crecca L 14½" (37 cm)

FIELD MARKS
Male's chestnut head has dark
green ear patch outlined in white

Female has mottled, dusky brown
upperparts; white undertail
coverts and belly

In flight, shows green speculum
bordered in buff on its upperwing

Behavior
An agile and fast-moving flier, this is the smallest
species of duck known as dabblers. Dabblers either feed
at the water's surface or upended, tail in the air and
head submerged, to reach aquatic plants, seeds, and
snails. The Green-winged has a specialized bill for
filtering food from the mud. Travels in small flocks
that synchronize their twists and turns in midair.

Habitat
Found on coastal estuaries and tidal marshes, and on
shallow lakes and inland ponds, especially those with
standing or floating vegetation.

Local Sites
Although the Green-winged nests farther north, it is
known to court and breed in late winter in the
freshwater pools of the Brigantine Division of the
Edwin B. Forsythe National
Wildlife Refuge.

FIELD NOTES A close relative of the Green-
winged Teal, the Northern Shoveler hen, *Anas clypeata* (inset,
left), has similar plumage, but is distinguished by her large,
spatulate bill. The drake (inset, right) is more easily distinguished
by his green head, white breast, and brown sides, though his
head will molt to brownish in eclipse plumage.

Breeding | Adult male

CANVASBACK

Aythya valisineria L 21" (53 cm)

FIELD MARKS
Breeding male's head and neck
are chestnut; back and sides
whitish

Female's and eclipse male's head
and neck are pale brown; back
and sides pale gray

Forehead slopes to long, black bill

Behavior
Feeds on the water in large flocks, diving deep for fish,
mollusks, and marine vegetation. Its heavy body
requires a running start on water for takeoff. Flocks fly
fairly high in lines or in irregular V-formation. Walks
awkwardly, but not often seen on land. Listen for the
male's croak and the female's quack.

Habitat
Uncommon in marshes, on lakes, and along
shorelines, sometimes quite far out. Builds nests above
water in thick marsh grasses.

Local Sites
The Canvasback is one of the more than 20 species of
duck to visit the Brigantine Division of the Edwin B.
Forsythe National Wildlife Refuge every year between
fall and spring. Keep an eye out as well for its similarly
plumaged cousin, the Redhead.

FIELD NOTES Sharing the male Canvasback's reddish head and neck, the male
Redhead, *Aythya americana* (inset), can
be difficult to distinguish in the field. Look for its grayer back,
tricolored bill of pale blue, white, and black, and for its yellow
eyes—the Canvasback's eyes are red. The two species share
much of the same breeding range and nesting locations.

Breeding | Adult female, left; Adult male, right

GREATER SCAUP

Aythya marila L 18" (46 cm)

FIELD MARKS
Male has black head with green
gloss; black neck, breast, and tail,
a barred gray back, and white
sides and belly

Female has dark brown upperparts, a white belly, and a bold
white patch at base of bill

Behavior
Most often seen wintering in large, floating flocks.
Dives down to 20 feet to feed on insects, mollusks, and
aquatic vegetation, using its strong feet to propel itself
underwater. Flies for the most part in straight lines
with strong, rapid wingbeats. Though mostly silent, its
eponymous call is a loud *scaup*.

Habitat
Found on large, open lakes and bays, and along
shorelines. Prefers saltwater environments.

Local Sites
Though the Greater Scaup winters along the entire
coast of New Jersey from Sandy Hook to Cape May and
into Delaware Bay, huge flocks congregate anually in
Raritan Bay between Sandy Hook and South Amboy.
Look for them there between October and mid-April.

FIELD NOTES With nearly identical
plumage in both sexes, the Lesser
Scaup, *Aythya affinis* (inset: male,
left; female, right), is best distinguished by its peaked crown; the
Greater Scaup has a smoothly rounded head. Look also for the
Lesser's shorter white wing stripe, which shows in flight. Another
indicator is the Lesser's thinner, narrower bill, with a smaller
black tip.

Nonbreeding | Adult male

LONG-TAILED DUCK

Clangula hyemalis Male L 22" (56 cm) Female L 16" (41 cm)

FIELD MARKS
Winter male is largely white;
breast and back blackish; stubby
bill shows pink band

Female has white underparts,
dark upperparts and cheek patch

Male's long, black tail
conspicuous in flight

Behavior
Tightly packed flocks careen low over the ocean as they move from place to place in winter. The Long-tailed Duck dives to forage at depths down to 200 feet. Can be identified by its loud, yodeling, three-part call of *ow-ow-owdle-ow*, which can be heard any time of the year from up to a mile away. The female also grunts and quacks from late winter through spring.

Habitat
Winters along coasts and on very large lakes. Breeds on bodies of fresh water in Arctic tundra.

Local Sites
Barnegat Lighthouse State Park at the northern tip of Long Beach Island is good for spotting Long-tailed Ducks. Head out on the jetty extending into Barnegat Inlet and scan the channel and ocean for wintering flocks. Island Beach State Park just north of Barnegat offers good views of winter flocks as well.

FIELD NOTES The Long-tailed Duck is the only duck that under-
goes two complete molts every breeding season, in addition to
the molt into its eclipse plumage. As each bird apparently follows
its own molting schedule, drakes seen on the same day in the
same area may appear quite different from one another.

Breeding | Adult male

BUFFLEHEAD

Bucephala albeola L 13½" (34 cm)

FIELD MARKS
Small duck with large puffy head,
steep forehead, and short bill

Male has large white head patch
and a glossy black back

Female has a brown head with
small, elongated white patches on
either side

Behavior
Often seen in small flocks, some birds keeping a
lookout on the water's surface while others dive for
aquatic insects, snails, and small fish. Like all divers, its
feet are set well back on its body to swiftly propel it
through the water. Migrates at night, riding favorable
air currents, attaining speeds up to 40 mph. Able to
take off straight out of water, unlike most other diving
ducks. Truly monogamous, Buffleheads are believed to
stay with the same mate for years and to faithfully
return to the same nesting site each season. Male's call
is a squeaky whistle, female emits a harsh quack.

Habitat
Found on sheltered bays, rivers, and lakes in winter.
Nests far to the north of New Jersey in boreal wood-
lands near small lakes and ponds.

Local Sites
Look for the small Bufflehead in winter at many coastal
bays from Raritan Bay south to Cape May.

FIELD NOTES In its boreal forest breeding grounds, this smallest
of the North American diving ducks nests almost exclusively in
cavities created by the Northern Flicker; a nesting site so tiny
that it is speculated to have influenced the Bufflehead's own
small size.

Breeding | Adult male, left; Adult female, right

COMMON MERGANSER

Mergus merganser L 25" (64 cm)

FIELD MARKS
Male has blackish green head, black back, white underparts

Female has chestnut head, white chin, gray back, white underparts

Both sexes have a long, slim neck, and a thin, hooked, red bill

Behavior
An expert diver, the Common Merganser gives chase to small fish underwater. A long, thin, serrated bill helps it to catch fish, mollusks, crustaceans, and aquatic insects. Flies low with rapid wing beats, following the course of rivers and streams. Harsh croaks can be heard from the drake; a loud, harsh *karr-karr* from the hen.

Habitat
Prefers open water on which to winter, and will remain as far north as space on lakes and rivers allows. Found also on brackish water. Nests in tree cavities or rock crevices in woodlands near lakes and rivers.

Local Sites
The Common Merganser nests in small numbers every year along the Delaware River, but far greater numbers winter on larger reservoirs throughout the northern half of the state.

FIELD NOTES The male Red-breasted Merganser, *Mergus serrator* (inset, left), has a blackish green head like the Common Merganser, but is distinguished by a shaggy crest and a streaked breast. The female and immature Red-breasted (inset, right and center), unlike the Common, have white fore-necks and grayish brown upperparts.

Breeding | Adult male

HOODED MERGANSER

Lophodytes cucullatus L 18" (46 cm)

FIELD MARKS
Puffy, rounded crest

Male's white head patches are fan-shaped and conspicuous; black bill, back, and tail; white breast with two vertical black bars; chestnut sides

Female brownish overall, upper mandible dark, lower yellowish

Behavior
Dives expertly, using its wings and feet to propel itself underwater. Serrated bill is good for catching fish; also feeds on crustaceans, insects, and plants. Known to join forces with other mergansers to hunt fish, cornering prey in small streams or shallow bays. Also forages for shelled corn on some wintering grounds. Takes flight directly out of water, and moves swiftly with rapid wing beats. Throaty grunts and chatter can be heard from these ducks year-round. A displaying drake will also emit a rolling *crrrooo*.

Habitat
Winters chiefly on fresh and brackish water. In breeding season, found on woodland ponds, rivers, and backwaters.

Local Sites
Found throughout New Jersey in fall and winter, also look for pairs in summer near the banks of the Delaware River in Delaware Water Gap National Recreation Area. They are known to take advantage of nest boxes designed for Wood Ducks.

FIELD NOTES The Hooded Merganser drake will often raise and lower his crest. The fan-shaped white head patch is most conspicuous when the crest is raised. In flight, the drake will flatten his crest so that the head patch shows only as a white line.

Nonbreeding | Adult female

RUDDY DUCK

Oxyura jamaicensis L 15" (38 cm)

FIELD MARKS
Brown-gray upperparts, pale
underparts with brown barring

Male has bright white cheeks,
female's cheeks crossed by single
dark line

Breeding male has black crown,
bright blue bill, rusty-red body

Behavior
Referred to as a "stiff-tail" from its habit of cocking its
tail upright, this small, chunky diver is noted for its
grebe-like ability to sink beneath the surface and
disappear, its stiff tail feathers serving as a rudder.
Adapted for diving, its feet are the largest relative to
body size of all ducks. With legs positioned far back on
its body, it can barely walk upright. Feeds primarily on
aquatic insects and crustaceans; eats little vegetable
matter. A generally silent duck.

Habitat
Found on lakes, bays, and salt marshes during
migration and winter. Nests in dense vegetation of
freshwater wetlands.

Local Sites
Look for Ruddy Ducks at the Brigantine Division of
the Edwin B. Forsythe National Wildlife Refuge, just
north of Atlantic City.

FIELD NOTES Unlike most ducks, Ruddy pairs form after arrival at
breeding grounds and seem to last only until incubation starts.
Nests are usually constructed over water in emergent vegetation.
Female lays largest eggs in relation to body size of all ducks.

Year-round | Adult male

WILD TURKEY

Meleagris gallopavo Male L 46" (117 cm) Female L 37" (94 cm)

FIELD MARKS
Male has dark purple, green, and
bronze iridescent plumage

Bald, blue and pink head,
red wattle

Male has blackish breast tuft

Female smaller, less iridescent

Behavior
A ground feeder, the Wild Turkey will roost in trees at
night. It can fly well for short distances when alarmed,
but prefers to walk or run. Male's characteristic display
during breeding season involves puffing out his chest,
swelling his wattles, spreading his tail, and rattling his
wings, all while gobbling and strutting. In spring,
male's gobbling call may be heard from a mile away.

Habitat
Largest of game birds, the turkey lives communally in
small flocks. Frequents open forests and feeds on seeds,
nuts, acorns, and insects found in grainfields and forest
edges. Females raise large broods, nesting in leaf-lined
hollows in brush or woodlands.

Local Sites
Look for the Wild Turkey in the woods along Pleasant
Plains Road at Great Swamp National Wildlife Refuge,
or in the eight miles of trails that intersect the refuge.

FIELD NOTES Like many game birds, the Wild Turkey has a crop,
a pouch in its gullet, that allows it to quickly eat and store its
food, then hide from predators. The food stays in the crop and is
digested later with the aid of grit and pebbles in the gizzard.

Year-round | Adult male

NORTHERN BOBWHITE

Colinus virginianus L 9¾" (25 cm)

FIELD MARKS
Mottled reddish brown quail
with short gray tail

Throat and eye stripe white in
male, buff-colored in female

Whitish underparts with
black scalloping

Behavior
A ground feeder, the Bobwhite forages for seeds, grains,
insects, and leaf buds. Feeds and roosts in a covey
except during nesting season. Nest is usually a woven
cover of pine needles, grass, and vegetation with an
opening on one side. When alarmed, a Bobwhite is
more likely to run than to fly. Male's call is a rising,
whistled *bob-white*, heard chiefly in late spring and
summer. A whistled *hoy* can also be heard year-round.

Habitat
The Bobwhite has the largest range of all North
American quail, though its numbers are currently
declining in New Jersey. It prefers farmland and open
woodlands with plentiful underbrush.

Local Sites
Look for the Bobwhite along wood edges and in the
open fields of Hutcheson Memorial Forest, a natural
research reserve owned by Rutgers University. The
university offers guided tours on most Sundays.

FIELD NOTES To keep warm at night, a covey of Bobwhites,
sometimes as many as 30, will roost on the ground in a circle,
with heads facing outward and tails pushed together so that
their bodies are in contact.

Nonbreeding | Adult

COMMON LOON

Gavia immer L 32" (81 cm)

FIELD MARKS
Blue-gray bill; slightly curved
culmen

Dark upperparts, pale underparts,
white around eye in winter

Black head and bill, white-
checkered back while breeding

Behavior
A diving bird; eats fish up to 10 inches long, which it
grasps with its pointed beak. Keeps its head level while
swimming. Forages by diving and swimming underwater, propelled mainly by large, paddle-shaped feet.
Can stay submerged for up to three minutes at depths
down to 250 feet. It is nearly impossible for the
Common Loon to walk on land.

Habitat
Winters in coastal waters, or inland on large, ice-free
bodies of water. Nests on large wooded lakes. Migrates
overland as well as coastally.

Local Sites
Both Common and Red-throated Loons can be seen
in winter just offshore from Island Beach State Park
and at Barnegat Lighthouse State Park.

FIELD NOTES The brick red throat patch
of the Red-throated Loon, *Gavia stellata*
(inset), is visible only in summer, during
breeding season. In coastal waters in
winter, the Red-throated can be
distinguished by the sharply defined white on its face,
which extends farther back than that of the Common Loon, and
by its habit of holding its thinner bill angled slightly upwards. In
flight, its neck will droop farther than the Common Loon's.

Breeding | Adult

PIED-BILLED GREBE

Podilymbus podiceps L 13½" (34 cm)

FIELD MARKS
Small, short-necked, big-headed,

Breeding adult brown overall

Black ring around stout, whitish bill

Black chin and throat

Winter birds lose bill ring;
chin becomes white

Behavior
The most widespread of North American grebes, yet
the Pied-billed is seldom seen on land or in flight.
When alarmed, it slowly sinks into the water, holding
only its head above the surface. Its bill allows it to feed
on hard-shelled crustaceans, breaking apart the shells
with ease. Pursues fish underwater and, once prey is
grasped in its bill, will eat it whole while still submerged. Lobed toes make the Pied-billed a strong
swimmer. Call is a loud *cuk-cuk-cuk* or *cow-cow-cow*.

Habitat
Prefers nesting around freshwater marshes and ponds.
Also found in more open waters of large bays and
rivers, where it dives to feed on aquatic insects, small
fish, frogs, and vegetable matter. Winters on both fresh
and saltwater.

Local Sites
Look for a Pied-billed Grebe on the surface of one of
the small lakes or ponds found throughout the Pine
Barrens of southeastern New Jersey.

FIELD NOTES Like most grebes, it eats its own feathers and feeds
them to its young, perhaps to protect the stomach lining from
fish bones or animal shells.

Immature | 2nd Year

DOUBLE-CRESTED CORMORANT

Phalacrocorax auritus L 32" (81 cm) W 52" (132 cm)

FIELD MARKS

Adult is black overall; facial skin and throat patch yellow-orange

Pale bill hooked at tip

Distinctive kinked neck when flying

Immature has a pale breast

Behavior

After locating prey, the Double-crested Cormorant can dive to considerable depths, propelling itself with fully webbed feet. Uses its hooked bill to grasp fish. When it leaves the water, it perches on a branch, dock, or piling and half-spreads its wings to dry. Feeds on a variety of aquatic life and plants. Soars briefly at times, its neck in an S-shape. May swim submerged to the neck, bill pointed slightly skyward. Emits a deep grunt.

Habitat

The most numerous and far-ranging of North American Cormorants, the Double-crested may be found along coasts, inland lakes, and rivers; it adapts to fresh or saltwater environments.

Local Sites

Wintering Double-crested Cormorants can be seen out over the ocean or drying their wings on the jetties at Barnegat Lighthouse State Park on Long Beach Island.

FIELD NOTES Despite its name, the crests on the head of the breeding Double-crested Cormorant are rarely seen in the field, especially in the case of the eastern subspecies found in New Jersey, whose crests are black and less conspicuous than the white crests of its western cousin. Juvenile birds are brownish above, pale below; particularly on the breast and foreneck.

Breeding | Adult

BLACK-CROWNED NIGHT-HERON

Nycticorax nycticorax L 25" (64 cm) W 44" (112 cm)

FIELD MARKS
Black crown and back

Two to three white hindneck
plumes, longest when breeding

White underparts and face; gray
wings, tail, and sides of neck

Immature streaked brown below

Behavior

Primarily a night feeder. Even when feeding during
daylight hours, it remains in the shadows, almost
motionless, waiting for prey to come within range.
Forages on fish, frogs, rodents, reptiles, mollusks, bird
eggs, and baby birds. Black-crowneds, high on the food
chain, are susceptible to accumulating contaminants;
their population status is an indicator of the quality of
their environment.

Habitat

This heron has adapted to a wide range of habitats,
including salt marshes, brackish and freshwater wetlands, and lakeshores that provide cover and forage,
along with reservoirs and flooded agricultural fields.

Local Sites

In summer, Black-crowned and Yellow-crowned Night-
herons forage nightly in the pools of the Edwin B.
Forsythe National Wildlife Refuge. Listen for their
short, low calls of *woe* or their gutteral *quok*s.

FIELD NOTES The adult Yellow-crowned Night-heron,
Nyctanassa violacea (inset), is also adorned with long,
white neck plumes. A buffy-white crown and cheek
patches, and a largely gray body, distinguish the Yellow-
crowned from its cousin, the Black-crowned.

Year-round | Adult

GREEN HERON

Butorides virescens L 18" (46 cm) W 26" (66 cm)

FIELD MARKS
Small, chunky heron with short
yellow to orange legs

Blue-green back and crown,
sometimes raised to form
shaggy crest

Back and sides of neck deep
chestnut, throat white

Behavior
Usually a solitary hunter, a Green Heron that lands near
one of its kind is likely to be attacked. Look for the bird
standing motionless in or near water, waiting for a fish
to come close enough for a swift attack. The Green
Heron spends most of its day in the shade, sometimes
perched in trees or shrubs. When alarmed, it may make
a show by flicking its tail, raising its crest, and
elongating its neck, revealing streaked throat plumage.
Its common cry of *kyowk* may be heard as it flies away.

Habitat
Found in a variety of wetland habitats but prefers
streams, ponds, and marshes with woodland cover.
Often perches in trees.

Local Sites
The Green Heron will stay at Great Swamp
National Wildlife Refuge quite late into the fall
before heading south for the Gulf of Mexico.

FIELD NOTES An innovative hunter, the Green Heron will stand at
the edge of shallow water and toss twigs, insects, even earthworms into the water as lures to attract unsuspecting minnows
into its striking range. This is one of the few instances of tool use
in the bird world.

Nonbreeding | Adult

TRICOLORED HERON

Egretta tricolor L 26" (66 cm) W 36" (91 cm)

FIELD MARKS

White belly and foreneck contrast
with dark blue upperparts

Maroon patches at base of neck,
light brown on lower back

Long, slender yellow bill with black
tip; yellow legs

Immature has chestnut hindneck
and wing coverts

Behavior

While foraging for food in ponds or marshes, sometimes stirs up sediment underfoot, but more often waits
for prey to come near. Occasionally chases small fish,
then uses its long, sharp beak to spear them. Prefers to
forage for its food alone, chasing other birds away from
its small hunting area. In flight, like other herons, the
Tricolored draws its neck into an S-curve. Calls include
an *aah* and a *kul-kul*.

Habitat

Common inhabitant of salt marshes and mangrove
swamps on the eastern coastline and the Gulf Coast.
Rarely found inland. Generally nests among a colony
in trees, either on islands or near water.

Local Sites

The freshwater pools of the Brigantine Division of
Edwin B. Forsythe National Wildlife Refuge are
good spots to scan for the Tricolored in summer.

FIELD NOTES The adult Little Blue Heron,
Egretta caerulea, is slate blue overall, lacking
the Tricolored's white underparts. In breeding
plumage (inset), the Little Blue Heron acquires
long, ostentatious, dark-purple plumage on its head and neck.

Breeding | Adult

SNOWY EGRET

Egretta thula L 24" (61 cm) W 41" (104 cm)

FIELD MARKS
White heron with slender black
bill and legs; yellow eyes, lores,
and feet

Breeding adult has upward-
curving plumes on head, neck,
and back; nonbreeding adult
lacks plumes

Behavior
An active feeder, the Snowy Egret may be seen running
in shallows, chasing after its prey of fish, insects, and
crustaceans. Also forages by stirring up bottom water
with feet to flush out prey. In breeding display, the
Snowy Egret raises its plumage, pumps its head up and
down, and flashes the skin at the base of its bill, which
turns from yellow to vermilion. Also during breeding
season, the generally quiet bird will bray gutturally,
pointing its bill straight up.

Habitat
Prefers wetlands and sheltered bays along the coastline.
Nests several feet up in trees among mixed colonies
including heron, egret, and ibis species.

Local Sites
Find both the Snowy and the Cattle Egret in the pools
and trees of the Edwin B. Forsythe National Wildlife
Refuge, north of Atlantic City.

FIELD NOTES In breeding plumage, the Cattle Egret,
Bubulcus ibis (inset), acquires orange-buff plumes,
easily distinguishing it from the Snowy Egret's
stark white plumes. The nonbreeding Cattle Egret
can be mistaken for the Snowy in flight. Look for its
yellow bill and legs, both of which are also considerably shorter than the Snowy Egret's.

Breeding | Adult

GREAT EGRET

Ardea alba L 39" (99 cm)

FIELD MARKS
Large white heron with heavy
yellow bill, black legs and feet

Breeding adult has long plumes
trailing from its back, extending
beyond the tail

Blue-green lores in high
breeding plumage

Behavior
Stalks its prey slowly and methodically, foraging in
shallow water with sharply pointed bill to spear small
fish, aquatic insects, frogs, and crayfish. Also known to
hunt snakes, birds, and small mammals. Occasionally
forages in groups or steals food from smaller birds.
Listen for the Great Egret's guttural croaking or its
repeated *cuk-cuk.*

Habitat
Common to both fresh and saltwater wetlands. The
Great Egret makes its nest in trees or shrubs 10 to 40
feet above the ground. Colonies may have as many as a
hundred birds. Occasionally breeds north to Canada.

Local Sites
Found annually at Forsythe National Wildlife Refuge,
the Great Egret can also be found hunting for fish or
small game at numerous other coastal sites.

FIELD NOTES Early in the breeding season, the Great Egret grows
long, ostentatious feathers called aigrettes from its scapulars. In
the late 1800s, aigrettes were so sought after by the millinery
industry that Great Egrets were hunted nearly to extinction. The
grassroots campaign to end the slaughter later developed into
the National Audubon Society. Today, loss of wetlands continues
to threaten the population of Great Egrets and other herons.

Breeding | Adult

GREAT BLUE HERON

Ardea herodias   L 46" (117 cm) W 72" (183 cm)

FIELD MARKS

Gray-blue overall; white foreneck
with black streaks; yellowish bill

Black stripe extends above eye

Breeding adult has ornate black
plumes on its head

Juvenile has dark crown; no plumes

Behavior

Often seen standing or wading along calm shorelines
or rivers, foraging for food. It waits for prey to come
into its range, then spears it with a quick thrust of its
sharp bill. Flies with its head folded back onto its
shoulders in an S-curve, typical of other herons as well.
When threatened, draws its neck back with plumes
erect and points its bill at antagonist. Emits an
annoyed, deep, guttural squawk as it takes flight.

Habitat

May be seen hunting for aquatic creatures in marshes
and swamps; it can also be found hunting inland, in
fields and forest edges. Pairs build stick nests high in
trees, in loose association with other Great Blue pairs.

Local Sites

Found year-round throughout most of New Jersey, the
Great Blue can be seen at any of the major birding sites:
Great Swamp, the Pine Barrens, Cape May, or Edwin B.
Forsythe National Wildlife Refuge.

FIELD NOTES The generalist of the heron family, the Great Blue
feeds on fish, snakes, frogs, crabs, shrimp, and insects. Less
tied to aquatic habitats than other species, it will also give chase
to small birds, nestlings, or even small mammals, such as mice
and woodchucks, which it often wets before swallowing.

Nonbreeding | Adult

GLOSSY IBIS

Plegadis falcinellus L 23" (58 cm) W 36" (91 cm)

FIELD MARKS
Chestnut plumage glossed with
green or purple looks all-dark
from a distance

Long, brownish decurved bill;
brown eyes, gray legs

Nonbreeding plumage is a duller
brown

Behavior
This wader's long bill seeks out crayfish and crabs
hidden in their holes. Also feeds on water snakes and
small fish. Flies in lines or groups with head, neck, and
legs extended beyond body. Nests communally,
sometimes within a few feet of other ibises, herons, and
egrets. A breeding pair will rub heads, offer grass or
sticks to each other, or engage in mutual preening. Its
guttural croak is a loud *ka-onk*.

Habitat
Freshwater and saltwater marshes, mudflats, swamps,
and flooded agricultural fields. Nests on a platform of
sticks and plants, on the ground or on the lowest limbs
of trees.

Local Sites
Look for Glossy Ibises at the Brigantine Division of the
Edwin B. Forsythe National Wildlife Refuge.

FIELD NOTES The Glossy Ibis is largely absent in the West,
replaced by the similarly plumaged White-faced Ibis, *Plegadis
chihi*. This is thought to be the result of two waves of migration
from the Old World: one prehistoric, which evolved into the
White-faced with its band of white around the eye, red lores, and
red legs; the other, perhaps as recent as the 1800s, which
remains indistinct from the Old World Glossy Ibis.

Year-round | Adult

BLACK VULTURE

Coragyps atratus L 25" (64 cm) W 57" (145 cm)

FIELD MARKS

Small, black, unfeathered head and hooked bill

Sooty, black plumage

Shows large white patches at base of primaries in flight

Gray legs, gray-white feet

Behavior

Soars to great heights, flapping its wings rapidly then gliding for short distances on flattened wings. Feeds primarily on carrion and refuse, for which its bald head is adapted, but is also known to occasionally feed on live prey. Feeds heavily when food is available, but can go many days without if necessary. A generally silent bird, it may make grumbling or hissing sounds when competing for food.

Habitat

Common in open country and near human settlement, where it scavenges in garbage dumps. Does not make a nest, but tends carefully to young in recesses of abandoned buildings, or in the cover of caves or hollow tree trunks.

Local Sites

Look for this vulture above the Pine Barrens and the agricultural fields of southwestern New Jersey.

FIELD NOTES The two-toned wings and red head of the more common Turkey Vulture, *Cathartes aura* (inset), distinguish it from its cousin. Not quite as adept at spotting carrion, and without a keen sense of smell, the Black Vulture will compensate by swooping down on a Turkey Vulture's find and claiming it as its own.

Year-round | Adult

OSPREY

Pandion haliaetus L 22-25" (56-64 cm) W 58-72" (147-183 cm)

FIELD MARKS
Dark brown above, white below;
female has darker neck streaks

White head, dark eye stripe, gray beak

Pale buff plumage fringing in juvenile

Slightly arched in flight, wings
appear bent back or "crooked"

Behavior
Hunts by soaring, hovering, then diving down and
plunging feet-first into water, snatching its prey with
long, lethal talons. Feeds exclusively on fish. Call a
series of clear, resonant, whistled *kyew*s. During breeding season, a male Osprey may call to draw a female's
attention to a prized fish hooked in his talons.

Habitat
Nests near bodies of fresh or saltwater. Its bulky nests
are built up in trees or on sheds, poles, or specialized
man-made platforms. Leaves most of North America
after breeding season, but returns early from Central
and South American wintering grounds. Uncommon
inland; found on all continents except Antarctica.

Local Sites
The Osprey builds its nest up and down the Atlantic
coast of New Jersey, from Sandy Hook, down through
Island Beach State Park and Edwin B. Forsythe
National Wildlife Refuge, to Cape May. Look for it in
September on its way south from the hawkwatch
platform of Cape May Point State Park.

FIELD NOTES Females tend to be larger than males, as in most
species of hawks. This is an advantage while nesting as females
do the majority of brooding and take larger prey than the males.

Year-round | Adult

BALD EAGLE

Haliaeetus leucocephalus L 31-37" (79-94 cm) W 70-90" (178-229 cm)

FIELD MARKS
Distinctive white head and tail

Large yellow bill, feet, and eyes

Brown body

Immatures mostly dark on body
and head; blotchy white on
underwing and tail

Behavior
Rock-steady fliers, rarely swerving or tipping on their
flattened wings. The Bald Eagle feeds mainly on fish,
but often on carrion and injured waterfowl, squirrels,
rabbits, and muskrats as well. Sometimes steals fish
from other birds of prey. A breeding pair locks talons
and cartwheels together through the sky in an elaborate
dance during courtship. Emits a squealing *kak-kak-kak*.

Habitat
A member of the sea-eagle group, the Bald Eagle most
often lives and feeds along seacoasts or near rivers and
lakes. It nests solitarily in tall trees or on cliffs.

Local Sites
Bald Eagles can be found soaring above the peaks of
the Kittatinny Mountains of northwestern New Jersey,
or at nest sites in Salem County.

FIELD NOTES The use of DDT and other chemical pollutants in the
United States greatly diminished the Bald Eagle population in the
East. Ingested with the fish in their diet, the pollutants caused
the birds' eggshells to be fatally thin. The pesticide bans of the
1970s have resulted in great strides in the birds' recovery,
moving the Bald Eagle from endangered to threatened status.

Year-round | Adult female, left; Adult male, right

NORTHERN HARRIER

Circus cyaneus L 17-23" (43-58 cm) W 38-48" (97-122 cm)

FIELD MARKS
Owl-like facial disk

Slim body; long, narrow wings

Long tail with white rump

Adult male grayish, white below; female brown, white below with brown streaks

Behavior

Northern Harriers generally perch low and fly close to the ground, wings upraised, as they search for birds, mice, frogs, and other prey. They seldom soar high except during migration and in exuberant, acrobatic courtship display, during which the male loops and somersaults in the air. Often found hunting in the dim light of dawn or dusk. Identifiable by a thin, insistent whistle or a high-pitched *kek-kek-kek*.

Habitat

Once called the Marsh Hawk, the Northern Harrier frequents wetlands and open fields. Nests on the ground. During winter, roosts communally on the ground, sometimes with Short-eared Owls.

Local Sites

Look for a Harrier from the hawkwatch platform of Cape May Point State Park. The best time is from September through November.

FIELD NOTES A Northern Harrier high overhead can look like a falcon when gliding, due to its long, broad tail; or like an accipiter, due to the rounded tips of its wings. Look out for its bright white rump, one of the most noticeable field marks of any of the hawk species.

Juvenile

SHARP-SHINNED HAWK

Accipiter striatus L 10-14" (25-36 cm) W 20-28" (51-71 cm)

FIELD MARKS

Adult blue-gray above, reddish brown
streaks on neck, breast, and belly

Squared-off tail with narrow white tip

Thin, bright yellow legs and feet

In flight, only short head
projection beyond wings

Behavior

Preys chiefly on small birds, often engaging in ambush
maneuvers or aggressive pursuit, even through thick
foliage and undergrowth. Flight consists of several
quick wing beats and a glide, its maneuvers assisted by
a long, rudderlike tail. A *kek-kek-kek* can be heard when
the bird is alarmed.

Habitat

Found in mixed woodlands; nests are substantial stick
structures found in tall trees. Look for it out in the
open during fall and spring migrations.

Local Sites

The Sharp-shinned is the most numerous species of
raptor to pass Cape May Point State Park's hawkwatch
platform on its way south, with sometimes
up to 40,000 birds spotted in a single season.
Look for it there in September and October.

FIELD NOTES Distinguishing the Sharp-shinned
from the Cooper's Hawk, *Accipiter cooperii*
(inset), is one of birding's most difficult
accomplishments. Both species are largely
brown as juveniles; blue-gray above, rufous
below as adults. The Cooper's is slightly larger,
has a more rounded tail, and a longer neck in flight.

Year-round | Adult

RED-SHOULDERED HAWK

Buteo lineatus L 15-19" (38-48 cm) W 37-42" (94-107 cm)

FIELD MARKS
Adult has reddish shoulders and
wing linings; pale spotting above

Dark streaks on reddish chest

Black tail with white bands

In flight, shows pale crescent
at base of primaries

Behavior
The Red-shouldered Hawk flies with several wing
beats, followed by a glide on flattened wings. Look for
it during fall migration, saving its energy by soaring on
rising currents of warm air, called thermals. Hunts
from low perches for snakes, amphibians, small
mammals such as mice, and an occasional small bird.
Call is an evenly spaced series of clear, high *kee-ah* or
kah notes.

Habitat
Prefers woodlands, especially moist, mixed woods
near water and swamps. Nests close to tree trunks, 10
to 200 feet up. Known to return to the same territory
for years, sometimes even passing nests along to
succeeding generations.

Local Sites
The Red-shouldered Hawk can be seen in October and
November, migrating south from the ridges of the
Kittatinny Mountains in High Point State Park.

FIELD NOTES Five subspecies of Red-shouldered Hawk occur
regularly in North America. The widespread eastern race,
lineatus, indigenous to New Jersey, is characterized by a brown-
streaked rufous chest. The immature of this subspecies has
brown upperparts, and a finely streaked brown and white breast.

Year-round | Adult light morph

BROAD-WINGED HAWK

Buteo platypterus L 16" (41 cm) W 34" (86 cm)

FIELD MARKS

Dark brown above; adult pale
brown below with rufous barring;
immature darkly streaked below

In flight, white underwings have
dark borders

Short, broad tail has black and
white bands

Behavior

In fall, migrates in large flocks, called kettles, often
composed of thousands of birds. Perches near water at
the edge of the woods, then swoops down on its prey of
amphibians, reptiles, rodents, small birds, and large
insects. Nests of the Broad-winged are built by both the
male and female in a process which can last up to five
weeks. Its call, which can be heard on breeding and
wintering grounds, is a thin, shrill, slightly descending
whistle of *pee-teee.*

Habitat

Nests in deciduous trees of eastern woodlands of North
America. Winters primarily in South America.

Local Sites

Look for kettles circling on thermals from Sunrise
Mountain of the Kittatinny ridge, in Stokes State
Forest, northwest New Jersey. A good time to watch for
them is in mid-September, after a cold front and while
a northwest wind is blowing.

FIELD NOTES A long-distance migrant, this smallest of the
eastern buteos will avoid long water crossings as much as
possible; instead, it will follow inland mountain ridges, gliding
upon energy-saving updrafts of warm air, called thermals.

Year-round | Adult

RED-TAILED HAWK

Buteo jamaicensis L 22" (56 cm) W 50" (127 cm)

FIELD MARKS
Brown upperparts; heavy beak

Distinctive red tail in adults only

Whitish belly with dark streaks

Dark bar on leading edge
of underwing

Immature has banded tail

Behavior
Watch the Red-tailed Hawk circling around and around, searching for prey, sometimes even kiting, or hanging motionless on the wind. Perches for long intervals on telephone poles and other manmade structures, often in urban areas. Will partially eat large prey on the ground, but more often carries small prey back to perch. Listen for its distinctive call, a harsh, descending *keeeeeer*.

Habitat
Seen in more habitats than any other North American buteo, from woods with nearby open lands to plains, prairies, and even deserts. Scan along habitat edges, where field meets forest or wetlands meet woodlands, favored because of the variety of prey found there.

Local Sites
The most widespread hawk on the continent, the Red-tailed can be found year-round throughout New Jersey, from the Kittatinny Mountains to Cape May, and in the Pine Barrens in between.

FIELD NOTES While perched, Red-taileds are easy to spot, but migrating hawks soar at altitudes up to 5,000 feet, appearing as nothing more than specks in the sky.

Year-round | Male

AMERICAN KESTREL

Falco sparverius L 10½" (27 cm) W 23" (58 cm)

FIELD MARKS
Russet back and tail; streaked
tawny to pale underparts

Two black stripes on white face

Male has blue-gray wing coverts

Female has russet wing coverts

Behavior
Feeds on insects, reptiles, mice and other small
mammals. Hovers over prey by coordinating its flight
speed with the wind speed; plunges down for the kill.
Will also feed on small birds, especially in winter. A
young Kestrel will even give chase to butterflies,
perhaps as a sort of target practice. Regularly seen
perched on fences and telephone lines, frequently
bobbing its tail. Has clear, shrill call of *killy-killy-killy.*

Habitat
The most widely distributed falcon, seen in open
country and in cities, often mousing along highway
medians or sweeping down the shoreline. Nests in tree
holes and often in barns using little or no nesting
material. A pair nesting in the eaves of one's barn is
considered a fortunate sign, though there has been a
major decline recently in the Kestrel's population
throughout eastern North America.

Local Sites
The American Kestrel is a frequently sighted raptor at
Cape May Point State Park's hawkwatch platform.

FIELD NOTES Sometimes called a "Sparrow Hawk," which is a
misnomer. The American Kestrel does not consume a significant
number of sparrows; rather it feeds mainly on insects and small
vertebrates, such as reptiles, frogs, and, occasionally, small bats.

Year-round | Female

MERLIN

Falco columbarius L 12" (31 cm) W 25" (64 cm)

FIELD MARKS
Whitish buff below with heavy
brown to black streaking

Males blue-gray above; females
and juveniles dark brown above

Strongly barred tail

Narrow black moustachial stripe

Behavior
A powerful flyer, a Merlin neither dives nor hovers, but
catches its prey in impressive bursts of speed while in
pursuit. Feeds primarily on large insects and small
mammals, but has been known to take birds of equal
size to itself, such as flickers, grackles, and meadow-
larks. Call is a repetitive *kee-kee-kee*.

Habitat
Found in a variety of habitats, but nests in open
coniferous woods or wooded praries. Most numerous
along the Atlantic coast during fall migration.

Local Sites
The hawkwatch platform at Cape May Point State Park
and the sand dunes of Island Beach State Park both
provide vantage points for watching the fall migration
of the Merlin and Peregrine Falcon.

FIELD NOTES The larger Peregrine Falcon, *Falco
peregrinus* (inset), returning south from the Arctic,
is distinguished by its "helmet," the black on its
crown and nape, which contrasts sharply with its
pale neck. Look as well for the largely brown
juvenile Peregrine (inset, right).

Year-round | Adult

AMERICAN COOT

Fulica americana L 15½" (39 cm)

FIELD MARKS
Blackish head and neck; slate
gray body

Small, reddish brown
forehead shield

Whitish bill with dark band at tip

Greenish legs with lobed toes

Behavior
The distinctive toes of the American Coot are flexible
and lobed, permitting it to swim well in open water
and even to dive in pursuit of aquatic vegetation and
invertebrates. It has the ability to tip its tail up and stay
submerged to feed. Bobs its small head back and forth
when walking or swimming; forages in large flocks,
especially during the winter. Has a wide vocabulary of
grunts, quacks, and chatter.

Habitat
Nests in freshwater marshes, in wetlands, or near lakes
and ponds. Winters in both fresh and saltwater. The
Coot has also adapted well to human-altered habitats,
including sewage lagoons for foraging and suburban
lawns for roosting.

Local Sites
The freshwater pools of the Brigantine Division of the
Edwin B. Forsythe National Wildlife Refuge are good
spots to scan for Coots in migration and winter.

FIELD NOTES Its body too heavy for direct takeoff, the American
Coot's lobed toes help it to "run" on water. Accelerating with its
wings flapping rapidly, it is able to gain the speed it needs to
take flight.

Breeding | Adult

BLACK-BELLIED PLOVER

Pluvialis squatarola L 11½" (29 cm) W 45"

FIELD MARKS

Roundish head and body; large
eyes; short black bill; dark legs

Mottled gray; white underparts in
winter and juveniles

Breeding male has frosted cap;
black and white spots on back
and wings; black face and breast

Behavior

Hunts in small, loose groups for invertebrates such as
mollusks, worms, shrimp, insects, and small crabs,
along with eggs and sometimes berries. Locates prey by
sight, runs across the ground, stops, then runs off
again. In this respect, a plover has a similar hunting
style to that of a thrush, such as an American Robin.
Listen for the Black-bellied Plover's drawn-out three-
note whistle, *pee-oo-ee*, the second note lower in pitch.

Habitat

This shorebird prefers sandy beaches, mudflats, and
salt marshes. Nests on the Arctic tundra. Rarely found
in interior regions.

Local Sites

Look for the Black-bellied in its winter plumage (noted
above) on the shorelines of coastal New Jersey. You
might also be able to spot one in breeding plumage
heading back up to the Arctic during spring migration.

FIELD NOTES Black-bellied Plovers are swift flyers, due in part
to their long, pointed wings. While observing their aerial acro-
batics, watch for white uppertail coverts, a barred white tail,
and black axillaries, the regions where the underwings attach
to the body. Note as well that juveniles of the species may be
gold-speckled above.

Juvenile

Charadrius semipalmatus L 7¼" (18 cm)

FIELD MARKS
Dark brown above, white below

Single breast band is gray-brown in winter, black during breeding

Short white supercilium

Juvenile has pale-fringed upper-parts and darker legs

Behavior

Sights prey with its large eyes, then runs on the sand, stopping to probe for mollusks, worms, crustaceans, and buried eggs. Flocks often congregate at sundown, roosting communally with their heads tucked into their feathers. Distinctive call is a whistled, upslurred *chu-weet*. Song is a series of the same.

Habitat

Common on beaches, lakeshores, and tidal flats. Nests in the Arctic. Winters on coastlines, but seen through-out the continent during migration.

Local Sites

The Semipalmated is a common winterer on the saltmarsh mudflats of the Brigantine Division of the Edwin B. Forsythe National Wildlife Refuge.

FIELD NOTES The endangered Piping Plover, *Charadrius melodus* (inset), which breeds locally along sandy beaches the length of the Jersey coast-line, is the same size as the Semipalmated and has in common with it a dark breast band and a black-tipped orange bill during breeding season. The Piping's back is paler than the Semipalmated's, however, and its breast band is often incomplete.

Year-round | Adult

KILLDEER

Charadrius vociferus L 10½" (27 cm)

FIELD MARKS

Tan to chocolate brown above; white neck and belly

Two black breast bands

Black stripe on forehead and extending back from black bill

Red-orange rump visible in flight

Behavior

Often seen running, then stopping on a dime with an inquisitive look, then suddenly jabbing at the ground with its bill. Feeds mainly on insects that live in short vegetation. May gather in loose flocks. The Killdeer's loud, piercing, eponymous call of *kill-dee* or its rising *dee-dee-dee* is often the signal for identifying these birds before sighting them. Listen also for a long, trilled *trrrrrrr* during courtship displays or when a nest is threatened by a predator.

Habitat

Although a type of plover—one of the shorebirds—the Killdeer prefers inland grassy regions, but also may be found on shores. Builds its nest on open ground.

Local Sites

Found year-round throughout New Jersey, you can find one in Johnson Park in New Brunswick, along the Raritan River.

FIELD NOTES If its nest is threatened by an intruder, the Killdeer is known to feign a broken wing, limping to one side, dragging its wing, and spreading its tail in an attempt to lure the threat away from its young. Once the predator is far enough away from the nest, the instantly healed Killdeer takes flight.

Year-round | Adult

AMERICAN OYSTERCATCHER

Haematopus palliatus L 18½" (47 cm)

FIELD MARKS

Large, red-orange bill

Black head and neck

Dark brown back

White underparts and wing stripe

Juvenile is scaly-looking above, with dark tip on bill for first year

Behavior

Feeds in shallow water alone or in a flock. It uses its chisel-shaped bill to crack an opening in the shells of clams, oysters, and mussels; it then severs the shellfish's constrictor muscle and pries the shell open. Also probes sand and mud for worms and crabs. Courtship consists of calls coupled with ritualized flights of shallow, rapid wing beats and displays of side-by-side running or rotating in place. Calls are vocal and variable, including a piercing, repeated whistle; a loud, piping call; and a single loud whistle.

Habitat

Coastal beaches, mudflats, and rocky outcroppings. Nests in a scrape or bowl-shaped depression in sand or grass, or on gravel and shells piled above the tide line.

Local Sites

Oystercatchers seem to favor the mudflats of Tuckerton salt marsh near Atlantic City or Stone Harbor Point in Cape May County. Bring a good set of binoculars as they are quite wary of approach by humans.

FIELD NOTES There are several good commercial recordings available of the American Oystercatcher; a useful tool, since their calls are as distinctive as their bills.

Year-round | Adult

BLACK-NECKED STILT

Himantopus mexicanus L 14" (36 cm)

FIELD MARKS

Glossy black, needle-thin bill

White below and around eyes

Very long red or pink legs

Males dark black from head, down back, to tail; female and juveniles tinged dark brown

Behavior
Tall and elegant, the Black-necked Stilt feeds quietly in small groups or by itself. Exceptionally long legs allow it to forage in deeper water than most shorebirds. As it strides gracefully through the water, it picks small organisms from the surface. When disturbed, stilts are very noisy, their sharp calls, *pleek-pleek-pleek*, piercing the air as they take flight.

Habitat
Breeds and winters in a wide variety of wet habitats, but partial to freshwater.

Local Sites
The Black-necked Stilt neither breeds nor winters in New Jersey, as shown in map above. It rarely appears around Delaware Bay and may wander up Delaware River as far north as the Camden area.

FIELD NOTES The American Avocet, *Recurvirostra americana* (inset), and the Black-necked Stilt, both rare in New Jersey, make up the two North American members of the family *Recurvirostridae*. The Avocet's bill is long, thin, black, and upcurved. Its gray head and neck in winter and its white scapulars set the Avocet apart from its cousin.

Molting | Adult

GREATER YELLOWLEGS

Tringa melanoleuca L 14" (36 cm)

FIELD MARKS

Long, dark, slightly upturned bill

Long, bright yellow-orange legs

Head and neck streaked brown

White-speckled, gray-brown back

White underparts slightly barred with brown

Behavior

A forager of snails, crabs, and shrimp; also skims water surface for insects and larvae. Sprints short distances in pursuit of small fish. Usually seen alone or in small groups, this wary bird sounds an alarm when a hawk or falcon approaches. Call is distinctive series of three or more loud, repeated, descending *tew-tew-tew* sounds.

Habitat

Winters in coastal areas of the United States and south into Mexico, frequenting a full range of wetlands, including marshes, ponds, lakes, rivers, and reservoirs. Breeds across the Canadian boreal zone.

Local Sites

The Greater Yellowlegs winters the length of the Jersey shore and quite far inland as well. Look for them at low tide along the Raritan River in Johnson Park, New Brunswick.

FIELD NOTES The Lesser Yellowlegs, *Tringa flavipes* (inset, from left: juvenile; winter; breeding), shares much of the Greater's winter habitat. Distinguished by its shorter, straighter bill—about the length of its head—it is smaller in stature and less wary in behavior. The Lesser's call is higher and shorter too, consisting of one or two *tew* notes.

Breeding | Adult

WILLET

Catoptrophorus semipalmatus L 15" (38 cm)

FIELD MARKS

Large, plump, with long gray legs

Breeding adult is heavily mottled; white belly

Winter plumage pale gray above

In flight, shows black and white wing pattern with black edges

Behavior

The Willet, like other shorebirds, wades in search of prey, probing through mud with its long bill. Feeds primarily on aquatic insects and their larvae. While generally protective as parents, Willets are known to leave unhatched eggs behind once the first young leave the nest. Its breeding call of *pill-will-willet* is the origin of its name; it may also be heard giving a *kip-kip-kip* alarm call.

Habitat

Nests in a variety of coastal wetlands during spring and summer months, sometimes within 200 feet of another Willet nest. Moves south in winter.

Local Sites

Like many other Atlantic Coast shorebirds, the Willet is drawn annually to breeding grounds in the saltmarshes of the Edwin B. Forsythe National Wildife Refuge. In fall look for the larger and paler *inornatus* subspecies arriving from the West.

FIELD NOTES During courtship displays, the Willet will show its black-and-white underwing bands, one of its most identifiable field marks. Keep an eye out as well for the Willet's white rump.

Nonbreeding | Adult

RUDDY TURNSTONE

Arenaria interpres L 9½" (24 cm)

FIELD MARKS
Stout bird with short dark bill;
short orange legs and feet

Winter adult brown above,
white below

Black-and-white neck pattern

Adult female is duller than male

Behavior

Uses its pointed bill to flip aside shells and pebbles in search of aquatic insects, small fish, eggs, mollusks, crustaceans, and worms. Vigorously defends its feeding territory by giving chase to any intruders. Call sounds like a low, guttural rattle, used readily to let other birds know of possible danger. Hence other larger shorebirds establish nests near this small sandpiper.

Habitat

Makes its nest on the ground on coasts of the Arctic tundra and migrates to milder, saltwater tidal areas, beaches, and jetties for the winter, taking advantage of the greater availability of invertebrates found there.

Local Sites

The Ruddy Turnstone can be seen on its way to or from the far north at any point along the Atlantic coastline of New Jersey.

FIELD NOTES In breeding plumage, seen in New Jersey in late spring, the Ruddy Turnstone's dusky brown back becomes a striking black-and-chestnut pattern; its black-and-white neck becomes more pronounced; and it develops a black-and-white striped crown. Year-round, a complex pattern of black, white, and chestnut is revealed on the wing when in flight.

Nonbreeding | Adult

SANDERLING

Calidris alba L 8" (20 cm)

FIELD MARKS
In winter pale gray above,
white below

Bill and legs black

Prominent white stripe and black
leading edge show on wing while
in flight

Behavior
Feeds on sandy beaches, chasing retreating waves in
order to snatch up newly exposed crustaceans and
mollusks, then darts to avoid the oncoming surf. May
be seen standing for a long period of time on one leg,
even though it lacks a hind toe. An excellent flyer, aided
by ample wing length and sharp, pointed wings. Flocks
wheel and turn together in the air. Call is a sharp *kip*,
often emitted in a series.

Habitat
Breeds on tundra in the remote Arctic and subarctic,
west from Hudson Bay. Migrates to spend winter on
sandy beaches throughout most of the Southern Hemi-
sphere, traveling sometimes as much as 8,000 miles.

Local Sites
The Sanderling is a very common shorebird from late
summer to spring at most New Jersey beaches. Look for
it chasing receding waves at the water's edge.

FIELD NOTES Just before departing in late spring for its Arctic
breeding grounds, this bird acquires a rusty red wash over its
head, mantle, and breast, dramatically brighter plumage than on
its wintering grounds, where its pale gray blends in with the
sandy environment. Look as well for the juvenile of this species,
which has a salt-and-pepper pattern of black and white spots.

Nonbreeding | Adult

LEAST SANDPIPER

Calidris minutilla L 6" (15 cm)

FIELD MARKS
Short, thin, slightly decurved bill
Gray-brown upperparts
Streaked brown breast
White belly and undertail coverts
Yellowish to greenish legs

Behavior
Forages for food with its stout, spiky bill. Feeds on worms, insects, mollusks, small crabs, and fish, in muddy, sandy, or shallow water. In its Arctic nesting areas, it confuses predators with a "rodent-run" display in which its feathers puff out, its wings droop, and the bird runs along the ground, squeaking like a rodent. The Least Sandpiper's call is a high *kreee*.

Habitat
Common in coastal tidal regions and wetlands with exposed mud or sand. Breeds in Arctic regions.

Local Sites
Found in migration along the Jersey shore, you may also see this shorebird foraging on inland river banks, such as the Raritan in New Brunswick, at low tide when mudflats are exposed.

FIELD NOTES The Semipalmated Sandpiper, *Calidris pusilla* (inset, from left: breeding; juvenile; winter), migrates through New Jersey in spring and fall. It looks and behaves much like the Least Sandpiper, but is distinguished by black legs, slightly larger size, and a heavier bill.

Nonbreeding | Adult

DUNLIN

Calidris alpina L 8½" (22 cm)

FIELD MARKS
Upperparts grayish brown,
breast washed with gray-brown,
belly white

During breeding, back reddish,
underparts offwhite, belly black

Long sturdy black bill, curved
slightly downward at tip

Behavior
Probes in shallows with a rapid up-down stitching movement of its bill, looking for insects, larvae, worms, snails, small fish, and crustaceans. Short neck makes it appear hunchbacked during feeding. This small but impressive flier can reach speeds of more than a hundred miles an hour during migration. Rapidly moving flocks move through the air in tandem. Distinctive call is a harsh, reedy *kree*.

Habitat
Stays north in the summer, breeding on hummocks or raised dry areas of the Arctic tundra. Migrates south to coastal areas for winter months.

Local Sites
Flocks of thousands of Dunlins visit Edwin B. Forsythe National Wildlife Refuge yearly. The best time to see them is October to April.

FIELD NOTES Sharing the Dunlin's black legs and slightly drooped bill, the Western Sandpiper, *Calidris mauri* (inset), in winter is a bit paler above and its breast coloring is not as prominent as the Dunlin's. The juvenile Western (inset, right), has rufous edges on its back and scapulars.

Breeding | Adults

Limnodromus griseus L 11" (28 cm)

FIELD MARKS
Long black bill

Distinct pale eyebrow

In winter, brownish gray above, white below, with gray breast

In spring and summer, spotted red and gray back, head, and breast

Behavior
Probes mud for insects with rapid up-down stitching motion of bill, often submerging head in water. Roosts in fairly large flocks and interacts with other species, including its close relative, the Long-billed Dowitcher, *Limnodromus scolopaceus*. The Short-billed's song is a rapid *di-di-da-doo*, and its alarm call is a mellow *tu-tu-tu*, repeated in a series.

Habitat
Prefers open marshes and mudflats along the coast. Nests on subarctic tundra and grasslands on the ground in piled-up bundles of grass and moss.

Local Sites
Southward migration begins early for the Short-billed, so you may spot a few as early as July in the Edwin B. Forsythe National Wildlife Refuge. In April and May, you can see them there molting from pale gray to bright rufous before their journey north.

FIELD NOTES The tertials and greater wing coverts of the juvenile Short-billed have broad reddish-buff edges and internal bars, loops, or stripes, creating a remarkable patchwork of patterns visible on the Jersey shore August through October. Those same feathers on juvenile Long-billed Dowitchers are unpatterned.

Breeding | Adult

LAUGHING GULL

Larus atricilla L 16½" (42 cm) W 40" (102 cm)

FIELD MARKS

Breeding adult has black hood;
white underparts; slate gray wings
with black outer primaries

In winter, gray wash on head,
nape, and neck

White crescent marks above and
below eyes; drooping red bill

Behavior

Forages for crabs, insects, decayed fish, garbage, and
anything else it can get, sometimes plunging its head
underwater or harassing beachgoers for popcorn or
french fries. Large gull flocks can be observed feeding
on deposits of horseshoe-crab eggs in wet sand. Flocks
often congregate around fishing boats, seeking scraps
or discarded offal. Name comes from characteristic call,
ha-ha-ha-ha, given when feeding or courting.

Habitat

Common along coastal regions. Nests of grass and
aquatic plants are found in marshes or on sand.

Local Sites

Found along the coast of New Jersey, Laughing Gull
nests are generally located on the bay side of New
Jersey's barrier islands. Stone Harbor in Cape May
County hosts the largest colony.

FIELD NOTES It takes three years for the Laughing Gull to attain
its full adult plumage. The juvenile has brown on its head and
body. By the first winter, although it retains brown wings, its
sides and back turn gray, with a gray wash on the nape. By the
second winter it has lost all brown, but still shows a gray wash
along the sides of its breast. Not until the third summer does it
develop a black hood, the sign of a full breeding adult.

Nonbreeding | Adult

RING-BILLED GULL

Larus delawarensis L 17½" (45 cm) W 48" (122 cm)

FIELD MARKS

Yellow bill with black subterminal ring

Pale eye with red orbital ring

Pale gray upperparts; white underparts; yellowish legs

Black primaries show white spots

Immature has a bicolored bill

Behavior

This opportunistic feeder will scavenge for garbage, grains, dead fish, fruit, and marine invertebrates. A vocal gull, it calls, croaks, and cries incessantly, especially during feeding and nesting. The call consists of a series of laughing croaks that begins with a short, gruff note and falls into a series of *kheeyaahhh* sounds.

Habitat

More common along the coast, but also a regular visitor to inland lakes and wetlands.

Local Sites

Widespread and abundant throughout coastal regions of New Jersey, the Ring-billed Gull frequents parking lots, shopping centers, and boardwalks of the Jersey shore where it forages for food amid the beachgoers.

FIELD NOTES The Ring-billed Gull and its partner in crime, the Herring Gull, *Larus argentatus* (inset), are two of the three most common gulls on the Jersey shore. Very similar overall, the larger Herring has a red spot on its lower mandible, rather than a black ring, and has pinkish legs and feet. It uses pavement to crack open clam shells dropped from 50 or 60 feet above.

Breeding | Adult

GREAT BLACK-BACKED GULL

Larus marinus L 30" (76 cm) W 65" (165 cm)

FIELD MARKS
Large gull; adult has large yellow
bill with red spot on lower
mandible

Black mantle and upper wing;
white head, neck, and underparts

White primary tips, tail, and
uppertail coverts; pink legs

Behavior
The largest gull in the world, the Great Black-backed
will bully smaller gulls and take their lunches. Also
scavenges on beaches for mollusks, crustaceans, insects,
and eggs; wades in water for fish; roots through
garbage for carrion and refuse; even takes birds as large
as cormorants. An increase in the number of garbage
dumps in coastal areas has led to an increase in the
Great Black-backed's population. On breeding
grounds, listen for a low, slow *keeee-aaaahh*.

Habitat
Coastal areas of eastern North America and large
inland lakes. Breeding range is extending southward on
Atlantic coast.

Local Sites
The Great Black-backed scavenges year-round along
the coast from the Raritan River to Cape May.

FIELD NOTES It takes four years for the Great Black-backed to
acquire full breeding plumage. In its first winter, it is checkered
pale brown overall with a black bill and an almost white rump.
By its second summer, it has a black back, a white head, and
a paler bill, but its wings and tail are still brown overall. The third-
winter bird resembles the adult, but still has some dark on its bill
and some brown in its wings and tail.

Breeding | Adult

ROYAL TERN

Sterna maxima L 20" (51 cm) W 41" (104 cm)

FIELD MARKS
Orange bill

Whitish overall; forked tail

Full black cap acquired briefly,
early in breeding season

White crown with black on nape
for rest of year

Behavior
Hovers, then plunge-dives 40 to 60 feet into water after
prey of fish, shrimp, and crustaceans. Roosts along with
other species of terns and gulls on sandbars, beaches, or
mudflats. Full black cap held only briefly in spring; at
other times, look for black only behind the Royal Tern's
eyes and on its nape. Small groups may cooperate in
finding prey; once a school of fish is found, the entire
group will soon congregate at that location. Calls in the
Royal Tern's large vocabulary include a bleating *kee-rer*
and a whistled *tourreee*.

Habitat
Prefers coastlines. Does not nest in New Jersey, but
birds visit the Jersey shore from colonies further south
during post-breeding dispersal.

Local Sites
Find Royal Terns in summer and fall on the beaches of
Island Beach State Park and elsewhere along the coast.

FIELD NOTES Sharing much of the same habitat, terns are
distinguished from gulls by their long, pointed wings and bill
and by their feeding technique, plunge-diving into water for
prey. Also, most species of tern have a forked tail.

Breeding | Adult

FORSTER'S TERN

Sterna forsteri L 14½" (37 cm)

FIELD MARKS

Orange-red bill with dark tip

Pale gray above; white below

Orange legs and feet

Long, deeply forked gray tail

Black cap on breeding adult; only around eye in fall and winter

Behavior

When feeding, the Forster's flies back and forth over the water, then plunge-dives to capture small fish. May also forage on insects, grabbing them in the air or from the water's surface. Often gives a one-note call, a hoarse *kyarr,* while feeding over water or during breeding season. Also emits a piercing *kit-kit-kit* cry.

Habitat

Wintering range in North America, mainly coastal, is along the Gulf and portions of the East and West Coasts. Also inhabits inland marshes and lakes where abundant fish and insects may be found. Migrates to the mid-Atlantic coast, Midwest, Pacific Northwest, and southern Canada to breed.

Local Sites

The Forster's Tern can be found in the summer, patrolling for fish in the canals of Edwin B. Forsythe National Wildlife Refuge.

FIELD NOTES An endangered species, the Least Tern, *Sterna antillarum* (inset), will nest on sandy beaches, including those at Cape May Migratory Bird Refuge. The Least Tern is considerably smaller than the Royal, with a yellower bill and legs and a white forehead. The Least Tern also shows a black wedge on its outer primaries in flight.

Breeding | Adult

BLACK SKIMMER

Rynchops niger L 18" (46 cm) W 44" (112 cm)

FIELD MARKS

Long, red, black-tipped bill

Black back and crown; white face and underparts; red legs

Female distinctly smaller

Juvenile mottled brown above

Winter adults show white collar

Behavior

Uses long, pointed wings to glide low over water while dropping its lower mandible to skim the surface for small fish. Once its bill touches a fish, the maxilla, or upper bill, snaps down to catch prey. Breeds in colonies on beaches, often sharing a site with tern species to take advantage of their aggressive defensive tactics. Makes a yelping bark in nesting colonies or in response to a threat. Pairs sometimes sing a *kow-kow* call together.

Habitat

Prefers sheltered bays, estuaries, coastal marshes, and sometimes inland lakes. Nests very locally in large colonies on barrier islands and salt marshes.

Local Sites

One of the few remaining areas in New Jersey where the Black Skimmer breeds is Stone Harbor Point in Cape May County. Watch from a distance, however; the birds are sensitive to human disturbance.

FIELD NOTES The Black Skimmer has a distinctive bill: As a feeding adaptation, the lower mandible is considerably longer than the upper. It also has an adaptive pupil, able to contract to a narrow, vertical slit. This capability is thought to protect the eye from bright sunlight glaring off the water's surface.

Year-round | Adult

ROCK PIGEON

Columba livia L 12½" (32 cm)

FIELD MARKS
Highly variable in its multicolored
hues, with head and neck usually
darker than back

White rump

Dark band at end of tail

Black bars on inner wing

Behavior
Feeds during the day on grain, seeds, fruit, or refuse in
cities and suburbs, parks, and fields; a frequent visitor
to farms and backyard feeding stations as well. As it
forages, the Rock Pigeon moves with a short-stepped,
"pigeon-toed" gait while its head bobs back and forth.
Courtship display consists of the male turning in
circles while cooing; results in a pairing that could last
for life. Characterized by soft *coo-cuk-cuk-cuk-cooo* call.

Habitat
Widespread throughout North America. Nests and
roosts primarily on high window ledges, on bridges,
and in barns. Builds nest of stiff twigs, sticks, leaves,
and grasses on ledges, rafters, gutters, or cliffs.

Local Sites
Introduced from Europe by settlers in the 1600s, the
Rock Pigeon is now widespread and abundant
throughout most developed regions of North America.

FIELD NOTES A highly variable species, the Rock Pigeon's colors
range from rust red to all white to mosaic, due to centuries of
selective breeding. Those resembling their wild ancestors have a
dark head and neck, two black wing bars, and a white rump.

Year-round | Adult

MOURNING DOVE

Zenaida macroura L 12" (31 cm)

FIELD MARKS
Small, buffy head with black spot
on lower cheek; pinkish wash on
neck in male

Trim-bodied; long pointed tail

Brownish gray upperparts, black
spots on upper wings

Behavior
Generally a ground feeder, the Mourning Dove forages
for grains, seeds, grasses, and insects. Aggressively
territorial, it gathers to roost in sheltered groves after
breeding. May breed more than one time each year. In
flight, white tips on outer tail feathers are revealed.
Wings produce a fluttering whistle as the bird takes
flight. Known for their mournful call, *oowooo-woo-
woo-woo*, given by males during breeding season.

Habitat
Widespread and abundant, the Mourning Dove is
found in a variety of habitats, but prefers open areas,
often choosing suburban sites for feeding and nesting,
including front-porch eaves.

Local Sites
Aided by widespread clearing of forests, the Mourning
Dove lives year-round throughout New Jersey.

FIELD NOTES The Mourning Dove, like the other members of the
family *Columbidae*, has the ability to produce "pigeon milk" in its
crop lining, which it regurgitates to its young during their first few
days. In appearance and nutritious content, the substance is
remarkably similar to mammals' milk.

Year-round | Adult

YELLOW-BILLED CUCKOO

Coccyzus americanus L 12" (31 cm)

FIELD MARKS
Gray-brown above, white below

Rufous primaries

Decurved bill with dark upper
mandible and yellow lower

Undertail patterned in bold black
and white

Behavior
This shy species slips quietly through woodlands,
combing the vegetation for caterpillars, frogs, lizards,
cicadas, and other insects. Recognized as an important
predator of harmful caterpillars. During courtship,
male will climb on female's shoulders to feed her from
above. Unique song sounds hollow and wooden, a
rapid staccato *kuk-kuk-kuk* that usually descends to a
kakakowlp-kowlp ending; it is often heard in the spring
and summer.

Habitat
Common in dense canopies of woods, orchards, and
streamside groves. Also inhabits tangles of swamp
edges. Nests lined with grasses and moss found on horizontal tree limbs. Winters in South America.

Local Sites
Look for both Yellow-billed and Black-billed Cuckoos
at Great Swamp National Wildlife Refuge.

FIELD NOTES Sharing not only habitat but
nests too, the Black-billed Cuckoo, *Coccyzus
erythropthalmus* (inset), is known to sometimes
lay its eggs in the nests of Yellow-billeds. It is best
distinguished by a dark bill and red eye ring.

Year-round | Adult

BARN OWL

Tyto alba L 16" (41 cm)

FIELD MARKS
White heart-shaped face

Dark eyes

Rusty brown above, cinnamon-barred wings

White to pale-cinnamon spotted underparts

Behavior
A nocturnal forager of mice, small birds, bats, snakes, and insects. Hunts primarily by sound, keeping one ear pointed upward and one downward, often in pastures and marshes. Wing feathers with loosely knit edges and soft body plumage make its flight almost soundless, effective in surprising its prey. Roosts and nests in dark cavities in city and farm buildings, cliffs, and trees. Call is a harsh, raspy, hissing screech.

Habitat
Distributed throughout the world, this owl has adapted to the activities of man and is found in urban, suburban, rural, and forest regions throughout its range. Nests at all times of year in various sites, including tree hollows, barn rafters, burrows, or cliff holes. Has declined recently in northeast North America.

Local Sites
The Barn Owl is a declining species in New Jersey, found very locally in a few cities and farmland areas.

FIELD NOTES Farmers enjoy the presence of these owls because they are such efficient hunters of mice. Note that the darker birds are usually females.

Year-round | Adult rufous morph

EASTERN SCREECH-OWL

Megascops asio L 8½" (22 cm)

FIELD MARKS
Small; with yellow, immobile eyes
and pale bill tip

Underparts marked by vertical
streaks crossed by dark bars

Ear tufts prominent if raised

Round, flattened facial disk

Behavior
Nocturnal; uses exceptional vision and hearing to hunt
for mice, voles, shrews, and insects. If approached while
roosting during the day, it will stretch its body, erect its
ear tufts, and shut its eyes to blend into its background.
Rufous, gray, and brown morphs exist, with the rufous
morph predominant in New Jersey. Emits a series of
quavering whistles, descending in pitch, or a long, one-
pitch trill, most often heard in winter and spring.

Habitat
Common in a wide variety of habitats including woodlots, forests, swamps, orchards, parks, and suburban
gardens. Nests in trees about 10 to 30 feet up. Also
known to use man-made nesting boxes.

Local Sites
A tremulous whistle will sometimes lure the Screech-
owl out of the underbrush of the Pine Barrens or Great
Swamp National Wildlife Refuge. Its call is rather easy
to imitate and the owl responds readily.

FIELD NOTES Like most owls, the Eastern Screech-Owl seeks out
the densest and thickest cover for its daytime roost. To find it,
search the ground for regurgitated pellets of bone and fur, then
look in the trees above. Also listen for flocks of small songbirds
noisily mobbing a roosting owl. They are often more likely to find
an owl than you are.

Year-round | Adult

GREAT HORNED OWL

Bubo virginianus L 22" (56 cm)

FIELD MARKS
Large size; mottled brownish gray overall

Long ear tufts (or "horns")

Rusty facial disks

Yellow eyes

White chin and throat

Behavior
Chiefly nocturnal. Feeds on a wide variety of animals including cats, skunks, porcupines, birds, snakes, grouse, and frogs; watches from high perch, then swoops down on prey. One of the earliest birds to nest each year, beginning in January or February, possibly to take advantage of winter-stressed prey. Call is a series of three to eight loud, deep hoots, the second and third hoots often short and rapid.

Habitat
The most widespread owl in North America, the Great Horned Owl can be found in a wide variety of habitats including forests, cities, farmlands, and open desert. Uses abandoned nests of larger birds, which it finds in trees, caves, on ledges, or on the ground.

Local Sites
The Great Horned can be found across New Jersey, especially in Great Swamp National Wildlife Refuge.

FIELD NOTES The Snowy Owl, *Bubo scandiacus* (inset), is closely related to the Great Horned. The Snowy is seen in winter only occasionally on beach dunes and coastal marshes in New Jersey.

Year-round | Adult

BARRED OWL

Strix varia L 21" (53 cm)

FIELD MARKS
Chunky owl; with dark eyes in
large head

Dark barring on upper breast;
dark streaking below

Barred tail

Lacks ear tufts

Behavior
Chiefly nocturnal, the Barred Owl's daytime roost is
always well hidden in deep woods. Has a wide variety
of prey, including small mammals, birds, salamanders,
frogs, snakes, lizards, fish, crabs, and large insects.
Catches, holds, and carries prey in its sharp talons. Its
call, the owl call most likely to be heard during the day,
consists of a series of loud hoots: *who-cooks-for-you,
who-cooks-for-you-all*. Also emits a drawn out *hoo-ah*,
preceded by an ascending, agitated barking.

Habitat
Prefers coniferous or mixed woods near rivers and
swamps; also upland woods. Uses abandoned nests
located in trees. Its range is increasing in Pacific Northwest, where it has interbred with the Spotted Owl.

Local Sites
Listen for the Barred's distinctive calls in Great Swamp
National Wildlife Refuge.

FIELD NOTES The Barred Owl, along with the Great Horned, is
known generically as a "hoot owl." It earns its nickname by
routinely using up to ten different calls. These calls include wails,
whines, squeals, even an eerie laugh. Imitation of its calls can
often result in the owl approaching and even responding.

Year-round | Adult

SHORT-EARED OWL

Asio flammeus L 15" (38 cm)

FIELD MARKS
Dark facial disk with pale edges

Yellow to yellow-orange eyes

Tawny plumage overall

Boldly streaked breast, paler belly

In flight, long wings show buffy
patch above, black wrist below

Behavior
Long, broad wings make this owl a graceful flyer, able
to hover even on windless days, and may be seen briefly
soaring. Active at dawn and dusk, hunts small mammals, especially voles; its population correlates directly
to the abundance of available prey. Sometimes hunts in
daytime over open fields, particularly on cloudy days,
and will occasionally add small birds and large insects
to its menu. Generally silent on wintering grounds.

Habitat
Widespread across North America, the Short-eared
favors grasslands, marshes, fields, and prairies.

Local Sites
Look for the Short-eared hunting in winter at dusk
over the fields and marshes of the Edwin B. Forsythe
National Wildlife Refuge, or in nearby Tuckerton.

FIELD NOTES Owls, though chiefly nocturnal lin their habits, will
hunt by day as well as night. Their nighttime hunts are usually
governed more by hearing than by sight. When food is scarce,
the Short-eared Owl must spend more time hunting, and is thus
more likely to be seen during daylight hours with the approach of
late fall and winter.

Year-round | Adult

CHIMNEY SWIFT

Chaetura pelagica L 5¼" (13 cm)

FIELD MARKS
Cigar-shaped body

Short, stubby tail

Dark plumage, sooty gray overall

Long, narrow, curved wings

Blackish gray bill, legs, feet

Behavior
Soars with long wings at great speeds, often in a circle, catching ants, termites, and spiders while in flight. Groups of Chimney Swifts may circle above a chimney at dusk before dropping in to roost. During aerial courtship, the suitor raises its wings into a V. Its call is high-pitched chattering.

Habitat
Builds cup-shaped nests of small twigs glued together with dried saliva in chimneys, under eaves of abandoned barns, and in hollow trees. Roosts in chimneys and steeples. Otherwise seen soaring over forested, open, or urban sites. Winters as far south as Peru.

Local Sites
Chimney Swifts can be seen best at dusk, flying at great speeds over the ponds of Stokes State Forest, or over the city of Cape May.

FIELD NOTES The Chimney Swift once confined its nests to tree hollows and other natural sites. Over the centuries, it has adapted so well to artificial nesting sites, such as chimneys, air shafts, vertical pipes, barns, and silos, that the species' numbers have increased dramatically. It is the only swift seen regularly in the eastern United States.

Year-round | Adult male

RUBY-THROATED HUMMINGBIRD

Archilochus colubris L 3¾" (10 cm)

FIELD MARKS
Metallic green above

Adult male has brilliant red gorget,
black chin, whitish underparts,
dusky green sides

Female lacks a gorget, has
whitish throat, grayish white
underparts, buffy wash on sides

Behavior

This species probes backyard hummingbird feeders
and flowers for nectar by hovering virtually still in
midair. Also feeds on small spiders and insects. When
nectar is in short supply, it is known to drink sap from
wells made in tree trunks in early spring by sapsuckers.
In spring the male Ruby-throateds arrive in breeding
territory before the females and engage in jousts to
claim prime territory. Once mated, females build nests
on small tree limbs and raise their young by
themselves. In addition to the hum generated by its
rapidly beating wings, this bird emits soft *tew* notes.

Habitat

Found in gardens and woodland edges throughout
most of the eastern United States.

Local Sites

Find the Ruby-throated drinking from summer flowers
and at hummingbird feeders throughout the state.

FIELD NOTES Hummingbirds and the flowers they pollinate
have evolved to meet each other's needs. Typical flowers
favored by the birds are narrow and tubular, the nectar
accessible only to a long bill or tongue. The hummingbird is
attracted to the flowers' bright colors; a sign, perhaps, of the
nectar within.

Year-round | Male

BELTED KINGFISHER

Ceryle alcyon L 13" (33 cm)

FIELD MARKS
Blue-gray head with large,
shaggy crest

Blue-gray upperparts and breast
band; white underparts and collar

Long, heavy, black bill

Chestnut sides, belly band in female

Behavior
Generally solitary and vocal, dives for fish from a water-side perch or after hovering above in order to line up on its target. Also feeds on insects, amphibians, and small reptiles. The Belted Kingfisher is one of few birds in North America in which the female is more colorful than the male, which lacks the female's chestnut band across the belly. Call is a loud, dry rattle; given when alarmed, to announce territory, or while in flight.

Habitat
Common and conspicuous along rivers, ponds, lakes, and estuaries. Prefers areas that are partially wooded.

Local Sites
Found all year diving for fish in the ponds and lakes of Great Swamp National Wildlife Refuge, and in Culvers Lake in Stokes State Forest, northwest New Jersey.

FIELD NOTES Pairs are monogamous and nest in burrows they dig three or more feet into vertical earthen banks near watery habitats. Both sexes carry out the work in building the nest, and they also share parenting duties for their clutches of three to eight. Mated pairs renew their relationship with each breeding season, with courtship rituals such as dramatic display flights, the male's feeding of the female, and vocalizations.

Year-round | Adult male

RED-BELLIED WOODPECKER

Melanerpes carolinus L 9¼" (24 cm)

FIELD MARKS

Black-and-white barred back

Red nape, extending onto crown only on males

White uppertail coverts

Central tail feathers barred

Small reddish tinge on belly

Behavior

Climbs tree trunks by bracing itself with stiff tail, taking strain off short legs. Uses chisel-shaped bill to drill cavities in tree bark for nest holes or to extract grubs and insects. Also feeds on worms, fruits, seeds, sap from wells made by sapsuckers, and on sunflower seeds and peanut butter at feeders. Call is a whirring *churr* or *chiv-chiv* that rises and falls, reminiscent of the whirring of wings.

Habitat

Common in open woodlands, forest edges, suburbs, and parks. Breeding range extending northward. Nests and roosts at night in tree cavities.

Local Sites

Look for both the Red-bellied and the Red-headed Woodpecker in Great Swamp National Wildlife Refuge.

FIELD NOTES The Red-headed Woodpecker, *Melanerpes erythrocephalus* (inset), shares much of the Red-bellied's range, including portions of southern and northwestern New Jersey, but is much less common. The adult Red-headed is identified by its bright red head, neck, and throat.

Year-round | Adult male

YELLOW-BELLIED SAPSUCKER

Sphyrapicus varius L 8½" (22 cm)

FIELD MARKS
Red forecrown on black-and-white head; chin, throat red in male, white in female

Back blackish; white rump and wing patch

Pale yellow wash on underparts

Behavior
Alone or in a pair, drills rows of evenly spaced holes in trees, then feeds on sap produced and insects attracted. Guards these wells fiercely from other birds and mammals. Also eats fruits, berries, and tree buds. Courtship ritual includes incessantly loud drumming by both male and female, *hoy-hoy* cries, and dual tapping at nest entrance. Though often silent, the Yellow-bellied sometimes makes a low, plaintive *mew* call, or an alarm call of *cheee-er*. Immatures more brownish overall.

Habitat
The most highly migratory of all North American woodpeckers, common in deciduous and mixed forests, where it nests, often near a body of water.

Local Sites
Look for the Yellow-bellied in migration perched on the small trees of the woodland thickets of Island Beach State Park just north of Barnegat Bay.

FIELD NOTES The bone and muscle structure of a woodpecker's head is an effective shock absorber; a necessary adaptation for a bird that spends its time drilling into hard wood. Similarly, a stiff tail and sharp claws help to maintain the bird's upright position against a tree trunk. Notice how a woodpecker's tail braces the bird; a much needed support to maintain its vertical perches.

Year-round | Adult male

DOWNY WOODPECKER

Picoides pubescens L 6¾" (17 cm)

FIELD MARKS
Red occipital patch on male only

Black malar stripe, cap, ear patch, and bill; black wings with white spots

White underparts, back, and outer tail feathers

Behavior
The smallest woodpecker in North America, it forages mainly on insects, larvae, and eggs. Also eats seeds, and readily visits backyard feeders for sunflower seeds and suet. Will consume poison ivy berries. Small size enables Downy to forage on smaller, thinner limbs. Both male and female stake territorial claims with their drumming. Call is a high-pitched but soft *pik*.

Habitat
Common in suburbs, parks, and orchards, as well as forests and woodlands. Nests in cavities of dead trees.

Local Sites
Both the Downy and Hairy Woodpeckers reside year-round in the Charles H. Rogers Wildlife Refuge near Princeton, but they are common throughout other wooded areas as well.

FIELD NOTES The larger Hairy Woodpecker, *Picoides villosus* (inset), is similarly marked but has a bill as long as its head and a sharper, louder, higher pitched call. Juveniles of both species show spots of white on the forehead and a crown streaked with red. Note the all-white outer tail feathers of the Hairy Woodpecker; the Downy's outer tail feathers are often barred or spotted black.

Year-round | Adult female "Yellow-shafted"

NORTHERN FLICKER

Colaptes auratus L 12½" (32 cm)

FIELD MARKS
Brown, barred back, cream underparts with black spotting, and
black crescent bib

Gray crown, tan face, red
crescent on nape, and, on male,
black moustachial stripe

White rump, yellowish underwing

Behavior
Feeds mostly on the ground, but is a cavity-nesting bird
that will drill into wooden surfaces, including utility
poles and houses. The Northern Flicker bows to its
partner before engaging in a courtship dance of exaggerated wing and tail movements. Call is a long, loud
series of *wick-er, wick-er* during breeding season, or a
single, loud *klee-yer* year-round.

Habitat
Prefers open woodlands and suburban areas with
sizeable living and dead trees. An insectivore, the
Northern Flicker is at least partially migratory, moving
southward in the winter in pursuit of food.

Local Sites
Found throughout the state, look for the Northern Flicker in
summer in the Pine Barrens of southeastern New Jersey.

FIELD NOTES Two distinct races make up the Northern Flicker
species. The "Yellow-shafted" Flicker, described above, is common in eastern and northern United States and shows yellow
wing linings and undertail coverts. The "Red-shafted," found
predominantly in the West, lacks the Yellow-shafted's red nape
crescent, shows red-orange wing linings, and the male has a
red, instead of black, moustachial stripe. Intergrades can be
found on the Great Plains.

Year-round | Adult male

PILEATED WOODPECKER

Dryocopus pileatus L 16½" (42 cm)

FIELD MARKS
Almost entirely black on back
and wings when perched

White chin under red moustache

Red cap full in male, less
extensive in female

Juvenile plumage browner overall

Behavior
Drills long, distinctively rectangular holes near base of
trees, then feeds on insects that sap attracts. Also digs
into ground, stumps, and fallen logs, feeding on car-
penter ants, beetles, acorns, nuts, seeds, and fruits. Call
is a loud *wuck* note or series of notes, but better known
by its loud territorial drumming, which sounds like a
tree being hit by a wooden mallet, and which can be
heard from a mile or more away.

Habitat
Prefers dense, mature forests; also found in woodlots
and parklands. Nests in a cavity excavated from a dead
or live tree, sometimes even in a utility pole.

Local Sites
The large Pileated Woodpecker can be found along
with at least five other woodpecker species in the
Delaware Water Gap National Recreation Area.

FIELD NOTES A close relative, the spectacular Ivory-billed Woodpecker, *Campephilus principalis*, distinguished by extensive
white wing patches, black chin, and ivory bill, is presumed to be
extinct. Formerly found north to the Ohio River, recent unverified
reports have led to search efforts in Louisiana and Arkansas, yet
results have been inconclusive.

Year-round | Adult

EASTERN WOOD-PEWEE

Contopus virens L 6½" (16 cm)

FIELD MARKS
Dark grayish olive above

Whitish throat and underparts, darker breast

Black upper mandible, dull orange lower mandible

Two thin whitish wing bars

Behavior
Perches on exposed lookout, searching for prey, then darts out to snare flying insects, such as beetles, moths, wasps, and bees. If threatened, defends territory from larger birds by flying at them and pecking. Song is a clear, slow, plaintive *pee-a-wee*, the second note lower, sometimes alternated with a downslurred *pee-yer*. Its calls, a loud *chip* and a clear, whistled, rising *pweee*, are often given together as *chip-pweee*.

Habitat
Breeds in a variety of eastern and midwestern woodland habitats. Winters in South America. Lichen-covered nests are well hidden in undergrowth.

Local Sites
The clear, whistled call of the Eastern Wood-Pewee is one of the first sounds at daybreak in summer at High Point State Park in northwestern New Jersey.

FIELD NOTES The Eastern Wood-Pewee is known to sit motionless for a long time on the same perch, sometimes spreading its wings or tail to preen. This is an important characteristic to distinguish it from *Empidonax* flycatchers, such as the Least Flycatcher, which flicks its wings and tail often and changes perches with great frequency.

Nonbreeding | Adult

EASTERN PHOEBE

Sayornis phoebe L 7" (18 cm)

FIELD MARKS
Brownish gray above, darkest on
head, wings, and tail

Underparts mostly white with pale
olive wash on sides and breast

Fall birds washed with yellow below

Juvenile has two buff wing bars

Behavior
The Eastern Phoebe flicks its tail downward when
perched, looking for flying insects to chase and snare in
midair. Also easts small fish, berries, and fruit. Among
the first spring migrants each year, its distinctive
eponymous song, a harsh, emphatic *fee-be*, accented on
the first syllable, announces the beginning of spring in
New Jersey. Call is a sharp *chip*.

Habitat
Common in woodlands, farmlands, and suburbs. Often
nests under bridges, in eaves, and in rafters, usually
near running water.

Local Sites
The Eastern Phoebe can be found giving chase to
insects flying over the steams of the Pine Barrens. It
builds its delicate cup nests in old buildings there.

FIELD NOTES The Eastern Phoebe has long been the subject of
scientific inquiry. The first bird-banding experiment in North
America, which provided information about life span, migration,
and nesting habits, was conducted by John James Audubon in
1840 when he attached a silver thread to the legs of several
Phoebe nestlings. Recent genetic research has revealed that a
male Phoebe other than the one tending the nest may father one
or more of the offspring.

Juvenile

EASTERN KINGBIRD

Tyrannus tyrannus L 8½" (22 cm)

FIELD MARKS
Black head, slate gray back

White terminal band on tail

Underparts white, pale gray wash
across breast

Orange-red crown patch visible
only when displaying

Behavior
Waits on perch until it sees an insect, then catches prey
in midair and returns to perch to eat. Feeds during
summer primarily on flying insects. Males court with
erratic hovering, swooping, and circling, revealing
otherwise hidden crown patch. Raspy call when feeding
or defending, sounds like *zeer;* also uses a harsh *dzeet*
note alone or in a series.

Habitat
Common and conspicuous in woodland clearings,
farms, orchards, and field edges. Builds cup-shaped
nest of weeds, moss, and feathers near the end of a
horizontal tree branch, sometimes on a post or stump.
Winters in South America, where it subsists mostly
on berries.

Local Sites
Look for the Kingbird's precise aerial manuevers while
hawking insects at Johnson Park in New Brunswick.

FIELD NOTES Living up to its Latin name, which means "tyrant of
tyrants," the Eastern Kingbird will actively defend its nest, sometimes pecking at and even pulling feathers from the backs of
hawks, crows, and vultures.

Year-round | Adult

WHITE-EYED VIREO

Vireo griseus L 5" (13 cm)

FIELD MARKS
Grayish olive above

White below; pale yellow sides
and flanks

Two whitish wing bars

Yellow spectacles and distinctive
white iris visible at close range

Behavior
Usually seen by itself, its thick, blunt, slightly hooked
bill used for catching flies and picking fruits and
berries. Known to sing into the heat of summer, when
other birds stay quiet, the White-eyed Vireo is characterized by loud, grating, jumbled, five- to seven-note
call, usually beginning and ending with a sharp *chick*.
The notes run together, the middle portion seeming to
mimic other birds' songs. Regional and individual
variations abound, but the standard, generic sequence
is *quick-with-the-beer-check!*

Habitat
Prefers to conceal itself close to the ground in dense
thickets, brushy tangles, and forest overgrowth.

Local Sites
The trails of Pleasant Plains Road in Great Swamp
National Wildlife Refuge are home to both
White-eyed and Red-eyed Vireos.

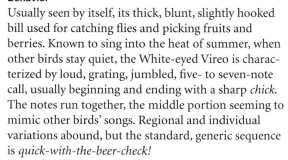

FIELD NOTES The Red-eyed Vireo, *Vireo
olivaceus* (inset), gets its name from the
adult of the species. The immature
(inset, right), actually has a brown iris. Its blue-
gray crown and white eyebrow bordered in black
distinguish it readily from the less common White-eyed.

Year-round | Adult

BLUE JAY

Cyanocitta cristata L 11" (28 cm)

FIELD MARKS
Blue crest and back

Black barring and white patches
on blue wings and tail

Black collar line on whitish
underparts

Black bill, legs, and feet

Behavior
Often seen in small family groups, foraging for insects,
nuts, and berries. Blue Jays are also known to raid nests
for eggs and nestlings of other species. A two-note
vocalization and a bobbing display may be observed
during courtship. Noisy, bold Blue Jays are noted for
their loud, piercing alarm call of *jay-jay-jay,* their
musical *weedle-eedle,* and their imitations of several
hawk species.

Habitat
The Blue Jay has adapted to fragmented woodlands,
parks, and suburban backyards. Builds nests of twigs,
bark, moss, and discarded paper or string in oak and
beech trees 5 to 20 feet up. Some birds are migratory,
while others are year-round residents.

Local Sites
Common across the state, the Blue Jay often favors
areas with an abundance of acorns.

FIELD NOTES A resourceful feeder, the Blue Jay is known to store
acorns in the ground for winter months when food is scarce. As
many of these acorns are never recovered, this practice is a
major factor in the establishment and distribution of oak forests,
further helping the jay's own cause.

Year-round | Adult

AMERICAN CROW

Corvus brachyrhynchos L 17½" (45 cm)

FIELD MARKS
Black, iridescent plumage overall

Long, heavy, black bill

Brown eyes

Black legs and feet

Broad wings and short tail

Behavior
Omnivorous. Often forages, roosts, and travels in flocks. Individuals take turns at sentry duty while others feed on insects, garbage, grain, mice, eggs, and baby birds. Regularly seen noisily mobbing large raptors such as eagles, hawks, and Great Horned Owls. Because its bill is ineffective on tough hides, crows wait for another predator—or an automobile—to open a carcass before dining. Studies have shown the crow's ability to count, solve puzzles, and retain information. Readily identified by its familiar call, *caw-caw*.

Habitat
Among the most widely distributed and familiar birds in North America. Lives in a variety of habitats.

Local Sites
Widespread throughout the state, crows can be seen almost everywhere.

FIELD NOTES The very similar Fish Crow, *Corvus ossifragus* (inset), is smaller than the American Crow with a high, nasal, two-syllable *ca-hah* call. It is found in coastal regions of New Jersey and along the Delaware River.

Year-round | Adult male

HORNED LARK

Eremophila alpestris L 6¾-7¾" (17-20 cm

FIELD MARKS
White forehead bordered by black band, which ends in hornlike tufts on adult males

Black cheek stripes, bill, and bib

Pale yellow to white throat and underparts; brown upperparts

Behavior
The only lark native to North America, it forages on the ground, favoring open agricultural fields with sparse vegetation. Feeds mainly on seeds, grain, and some insects. Seldom alights on trees or bushes. On the ground, the Horned Lark walks or runs, rather than hops. Outside breeding season, these birds organize into flocks. Song is a weak twittering; calls include a high *tsee-ee* or *tsee-titi.*

Habitat
Prefers dirt fields, sod farms, airports, gravel ridges, and shores. Uses its bill and feet with long hind claws to create shallow depressions for nesting.

Local Sites
Horned Larks are common in winter, with a number remaining to breed as well. A good place to spot them in fall and winter is Barnegat Lighthouse State Park.

FIELD NOTES During courtship, the male Horned Lark performs a spectacular flight display, ascending several hundred feet into the air, circling and singing for a bit, then plummeting headfirst toward the ground and flaring his wings open at the last second.

Year-round | Adult male

PURPLE MARTIN

Progne subis L 8" (20 cm)

FIELD MARKS

Male is dark, glossy purplish blue

Female has bluish gray upper-parts; grayish breast and belly

Forked tail

Dark eyes, bill, legs, and feet

Juvenile gray below

Behavior

Forages almost exclusively in flight, darting for wasps, bees, dragonflies, winged ants, and other large insects. Long, sharply pointed wings and a substantial tail allow it graceful maneuverability in the air, but feet and legs are small, so it walks with a weak, shuffling gait. Capable of drinking, even bathing, in flight by skimming just over water's surface and dipping bill, or breast, into water. Song is a series of liquid, gurgling notes.

Habitat

Common in summer in open habitat where it nests almost exclusively in man-made multi-dwelling martin houses. Winters in South America.

Local Sites

Purple Martins return annually to nest boxes set up at Forsythe Refuge and Cape May Point State Park.

FIELD NOTES Eastern Purple Martins are highly dependent on man-made nesting houses, which can hold many pairs of breeding adults. The tradition of making Martin houses from hollowed gourds originated with Native Americans, who found that this sociable bird helped reduce insects around villages and crops. The practice was adopted by colonists as well. Martins have accordingly prospered for many generations.

Breeding | Adult male

TREE SWALLOW

Tachycineta bicolor L 5¾" (15 cm)

FIELD MARKS
Dark, glossy, greenish blue above;
white below

Slightly notched tail

Long, pointed, blackish wings

Juvenile gray-brown above

Behavior
Abundant and widespread, with uncanny ability to
adapt to divergent environments. Often seen in huge
flocks, especially during fall migration or perched in
long rows on branches and wires. Darts to catch insects
in flight, but changes to a diet of berries or plant buds
during colder months, when insects are less abundant.
The Tree Swallow even preens itself in flight. Song is a
rapid, repeated *chi-veet*.

Habitat
Common to wooded habitats near water, or where
dead trees provide nest holes in fields, marshes, or
towns. Also nests in fence posts, barn eaves, and man-
made birdhouses.

Local Sites
Find Tree Swallows in summer darting above streams
and ponds the state over, especially at Lily Lake in
Forsythe Refuge. In early autumn, large numbers
congregate at barrier islands and marshes.

FIELD NOTES Many Tree Swallows spend the winter along the
southern Atlantic and Gulf Coasts, the rest further south. Note as
well that the juvenile is gray-brown above with a dusky wash on
its breast.

Year-round | Adult

BARN SWALLOW

Hirundo rustica L 6¾" (17 cm)

FIELD MARKS

Long, deeply forked tail

Reddish brown forehead and throat

Dark blue-black breast band

Iridescent blue upperparts

Cinnamon to buff underparts

Behavior

An exuberant flyer, the Barn Swallow is often seen in small flocks skimming low over the surface of a field or pond, taking insects in midair. Will follow tractors and lawn mowers to feed on flushed insects, many of which are harmful to crops. An indicator of coming storms, as barometric pressure changes cause the bird to fly lower to the ground. Call is a short, repeated *wit-wit.*

Habitat

Frequents open farms and fields, especially near water. Has adapted to humans to the extent that it now nests almost exclusively in structures such as barns, bridges, culverts, and garages. Nest is bowl-shaped, made of mud, and lined with grass and feathers.

Local Sites

The Barn Swallow can be found along streams in the state as early as April. Departs in fall on lengthy flight to wintering grounds in South America.

FIELD NOTES The juvenile Barn Swallow has pale underparts and a noticeably shorter tail, still with characteristic fork. Female is generally duller overall. The world's most widely distributed swallow, it is common and abundant throughout Europe and Asia and winters in southern Africa and South America.

Year-round | Adult

CAROLINA CHICKADEE

Poecile carolinensis L 4¾" (12 cm)

FIELD MARKS
Black cap and bib

White cheeks, gray upperparts

Whitish underparts, with buff-gray
wash on flanks and lower belly

Short black bill, blackish legs

Short, slightly notched tail

Behavior
Seldom descends to ground, energetically forages
among leaves and twigs for moths, caterpillars, and
insects. Often hangs upside down to glean underside of
foliage. Visits backyard feeders for seeds and suet. After
breeding season it joins in mixed foraging flocks with
nuthatches, titmice, Downy Woodpeckers, and other
small birds. Best distinguished from Black-capped
Chickadee by call, a higher, faster version of *chick-a-
dee-dee-dee*. Song is a four-note whistle, *fee-bee fee-bay*.

Habitat
Woodland edges and clearings, oak forests, wooded city
parks, and suburban yards. Nests in old woodpecker
holes, man-made nesting boxes, and natural crevices.

Local Sites
The ranges of the Carolina and Black-capped
Chickadee just barely meet at the Charles H. Rogers
Wildlife Refuge near Princeton in Mercer County.

FIELD NOTES The Black-capped Chickadee,
Poecile atricapillus (inset), has plumage nearly
identical to the Carolina's, but its wing
coverts are edged in white; also, its call is
slower. Its range is north and west of the Carolina's;
they hybridize where their ranges narrowly overlap.

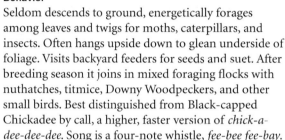

Year-round | Adult

TUFTED TITMOUSE

Baeolophus bicolor L 6¼" (16 cm)

FIELD MARKS
Gray crest; blackish forehead

Gray upperparts; whitish
underparts

Russet wash on sides

Juvenile has brownish forehead
and pale crest

Behavior
Very active forager in trees, seeking insects, sometimes
hanging upside down while feeding. May also be seen
holding a nut with its feet and pounding it with its bill.
A common visitor to backyard feeders, especially fond
of sunflower seeds and suet. Stores surplus food under-
ground. Male feeds female in courtship. Primary song
is a loud, whistled *peter-peter-peter,* but it also employs
up to ten other calls, which it uses to keep foraging
groups together.

Habitat
Open forests, woodlands, groves, and orchards, as well
as urban and suburban parks with large trees and
shrubs. Nests in natural cavities, woodpecker holes,
man-made boxes, sometimes in fence posts near open
pastures surrounded by wooded areas.

Local Sites
Listen for the noisy calls of Tufted Titmice almost
everywhere. Try the Charles H. Rogers Wildlife Refuge.

FIELD NOTES Unintimidated by proximity to humans, the Tufted
Titmouse will fly toward people who make a squeaking sound or
pish to attract birds. It is even known to swoop down and pluck
hair directly from a human's scalp for use in its nest.

Year-round | Adult

BROWN CREEPER

Certhia americana L 5¼" (13 cm)

FIELD MARKS
Streaked brown upperparts
White underparts
Thin, pointed, decurved bill
White eyebrow stripe
Sharp claws

Behavior
Small, quiet, and unassuming, the Creeper is easy to over-look. Probes the bark of a tree for insects and larvae as it spirals upward along the trunk, then flies down to a lower spot on a nearby tree and repeats the procedure. Like a woodpecker, the Creeper props itself with its stiff tail as it climbs. Usually solitary, it may be seen in winter flocks of titmice and nuthatches. Call is a soft, sibilant *see;* song a high-pitched, variable *see-see-titi-see.*

Habitat
Tucks its nest of twigs, bark, and moss in crevices between the bark and trunk of trees in coniferous, mixed, or swampy forests. Moves south in the fall.

Local Sites
Check year-round for the Creeper in forests of the Pine Barrens and Delaware Water Gap National Recreation Area. In October, they may be found in the woodland thickets of Island Beach State Park.

FIELD NOTES The Brown Creeper is fairly common, but quite difficult to spot. It defends itself from predators by pressing its body against a tree trunk, spreading out its wings and tail, camouflaging itself by remaining motionless for long stretches. Listen closely for its soft, high-pitched, almost inaudible call.

Year-round | Adult male

RED-BREASTED NUTHATCH

Sitta canadensis L 4½" (11 cm)

FIELD MARKS
Rust-colored below, blue-gray
above

Black cap; white eyebrow; black
postocular stripe; white cheeks

Female, juvenile have duller head,
paler underparts

Behavior
Climbs up and down conifer trunks, small branches,
and outer twigs often headfirst, foraging for seeds, nuts,
and insects. Often wedges a nut into a bark crevice,
then pounds it with its bill to break open the shell.
Smears pine pitch at nest entrance, apparently to ward
off predators. High-pitched, nasal call is a repeated *ank.*

Habitat
Northern and subalpine conifer and mixed forests.
Range is expanding southward in the East. Winter
range varies each year, as the nuthatch is known to
remain in its breeding range as long as food is available.

Local Sites
The Red-breasted Nuthatch is a resident of the forests
of Delaware Water Gap National Recreation Area. In
winter, look for it throughout the state foraging along
with chickadees, kinglets, and creepers.

FIELD NOTES In winter, the Red-breasted often
joins a mixed-species foraging group with the
White-breasted Nuthatch, *Sitta carolinensis*
(inset; male, top). Though similar in behavior, the
more widespread White-breasted is noticeably
larger and has an all-white face and breast.

Year-round | Adult

CAROLINA WREN

Thryothorus ludovicianus L 5½" (14 cm)

FIELD MARKS
Deep rusty brown above with
dark brown bars

Warm buff below

Prominent white eye stripe

White chin and throat

Long, slightly decurved bill

Behavior

Pokes into every nook and cranny near the ground
with its decurved bill, looking for insects, spiders,
snails, millipedes, fruits, berries, and seeds. May also eat
small lizards and tree frogs. A pair stays together in its
territory throughout the year. From its perch at any
time of day or season, male sings melodious *tea-kettle
tea-kettle tea-kettle* or *cheery-cheery-cheery,* to which
female often responds with a growl of *t-shihrrr.*

Habitat

Widespread and common in underbrush of moist
woodlands and swamps, and around human habitation
on farms and in wooded suburbs. Nests in open cavities of suitable size, including woodpecker holes, barn
rafters, mailboxes, flowerpots, even boots left outside.

Local Sites

The Carolina Wren can be heard year-
round, especially in southern New Jersey.

FIELD NOTES The most widespread of North
American wrens is the House Wren,
Troglodytes aedon (inset). It is smaller and
grayer than the Carolina, with a less prominent eye
stripe and a lively, whistled song. Listen for its melodious trilling in summer in Great Swamp National Wildlife Refuge.

Year-round | Adult

WINTER WREN

Troglodytes troglodytes L 4" (10 cm)

FIELD MARKS
Short, stubby tail; stocky body

Dark brown overall with faint
barring above

Heavily barred tail, flanks,
and underparts

Buff chin and throat

Behavior
Its rapid, cascading song belies the size of this small
songbird. Tends to be solitary when not paired for
breeding. An active ground feeder, it constantly bobs its
head and flicks its tail as it gleans insects and berries
from brush and dense thickets. Perches with its head
bobbing up and down as it sings a melodious series of
trills; call is a *kelp-kelp*.

Habitat
Secretive inhabitant of dense brush in moist woods,
especially along stream banks.

Local Sites
Look for the Winter Wren flitting around dense cover,
searching brush piles for insects in riparian regions of
Delaware Water Gap National Recreation Area,
especially during winter months.

FIELD NOTES Commonly hidden in the
reedy marshes and cattail swamps of
coastal New Jersey, the Marsh Wren,
Cistothorus palustris (inset), reveals its
location only with its constant, abrasive call
of *tsuk-tsuk*. Like the Winter Wren, it is dark
brown overall, but has a prominent white eye
stripe and its mantle is streaked black-and-white.

Year-round | Adult male

RUBY-CROWNED KINGLET

Regulus calendula L 4¼" (11 cm)

FIELD MARKS
Olive green above; dusky below

Male's red crown patch seldom
visible except when agitated

Yellow-edged plumage on wings

Two white wing bars

Short black bill; white eye ring

Behavior
Often seen foraging in mixed-species flocks, the Ruby-
crowned Kinglet often flicks its wings as it searches for
insects and their eggs or larvae on tree trunks, branches, and foliage. May also give chase to flying insects or
drink sap from tree wells drilled by sapsuckers. Calls
include a scolding *ji-dit;* song consists of several high,
thin *tsee* notes, followed by descending *tew* notes, ending with a trilled three-note phrase.

Habitat
Common in coniferous and mixed woodlands and
thickets across North America. Highly migratory.

Local Sites
October is the best time to look for this small songbird
on its way farther south. Try the woodland thickets of
Island Beach State Park and Cape May.

FIELD NOTES A close relative of the Ruby-
crowned, the Golden-crowned Kinglet, *Regulus
satrapa* (inset), can be found in winter as it
forages high up in trees. The Golden-crowned is
set apart by its yellow crown patch and its white
eyebrow stripe. An agitated male (inset, left) will
flash a brilliant orange tuft within its yellow crown patch.

Breeding | Adult male

BLUE-GRAY GNATCATCHER

Polioptila caerulea L 4¼" (11 cm)

FIELD MARKS

Male is blue-gray above, female is grayer; both are white below

Black line on sides of crown in male, breeding plumage only

Long, black tail with white outer feathers

Behavior

Often seen near branch tips, the gnatcatcher scours deciduous tree limbs and leaves for small insects, spiders, eggs, and larvae. Sometimes captures prey in flight and may hover briefly. Distinguished by its high-pitched buzz while feeding or breeding. Also emits a querulous *pwee,* intoned like a question. Known to imitate other birds' songs, a surprise to birders expecting this only from mockingbirds and thrashers.

Habitat

Favors woodlands and thickets. Male and female together make a cuplike nest of plant fibers, spider webs, moss, and lichen. Winters in southern U.S., Mexico, and Central America.

Local Sites

The Blue-gray Gnatcatcher nests near streams in the Pine Barrens, or lakes in Stokes State Forest.

FIELD NOTES Like many of the smaller species, gnatcatchers hatch altricial—naked and unable to see, requiring complete parental care. Young are fed in the nest for about two weeks, then outside for an additional period of time. Avoid disturbing a nest site, as it may sometimes cause the couple to abandon it and rebuild elsewhere.

Year-round | Adult male

EASTERN BLUEBIRD

Sialia sialis L 7" (18 cm)

FIELD MARKS
Chestnut throat, breast, flanks,
and sides of neck

White belly and undertail coverts

Male is bright blue above

Female is grayer blue above,
duller below

Behavior
Hunts from an elevated perch in the open, dropping to
the ground to seize crickets, grasshoppers, and spiders.
The Eastern Bluebird has been observed pouncing on
prey it has spotted from as much as 130 feet away. In
winter, may form small flocks and roost communally in
tree cavities or nest boxes by night. During courtship,
the male shows the vivid coloring on its side during
wing-waving displays beside a chosen nesting site. Call
note is a musical, rising *chur-lee,* extended in song to
chur chur-lee chur-lee.

Habitat
Found in open woodlands, meadows, farmlands, and
orchards. Nests with grass, stems, twigs, and needles in
holes in trees and posts, and in nest boxes.

Local Sites
The bluebird frequents open areas of the Great Swamp
National Wildlife Refuge.

FIELD NOTES The Eastern Bluebird's serious decline in recent
decades is due largely to competition for nesting sites with two
introduced species, the European Starling and the House
Sparrow. Specially designed nesting boxes provided by
concerned birders have contributed to a promising comeback.

Year-round | Adult female

AMERICAN ROBIN

Turdus migratorius L 10" (25 cm)

FIELD MARKS
Gray-brown above with darker head and tail

Brick red underparts, paler in female

White throat and lower belly

Broken white eye ring; yellow bill

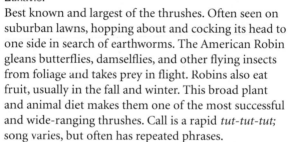

Behavior
Best known and largest of the thrushes. Often seen on suburban lawns, hopping about and cocking its head to one side in search of earthworms. The American Robin gleans butterflies, damselflies, and other flying insects from foliage and takes prey in flight. Robins also eat fruit, usually in the fall and winter. This broad plant and animal diet makes them one of the most successful and wide-ranging thrushes. Call is a rapid *tut-tut-tut;* song varies, but often has repeated phrases.

Habitat
Common and widespread, the American Robin forages on lawns and nests in shrubs, trees, and even on sheltered windowsills. Winters in moist woodlands, swamps, suburbs, and parks.

Local Sites
Look for robins almost anywhere in the state, including your own backyard.

FIELD NOTES The juvenile robin has a paler breast, like the female of the species, but its underparts are heavily spotted with brown. Look as well for spots of white on its back and wings.

Year-round | Adult

GRAY CATBIRD

Dumetella carolinensis L 8½" (22 cm)

FIELD MARKS
Dark gray overall

Black cap

Long, black tail, often cocked

Undertail coverts chestnut

Short, dark bill

Behavior
Stays low in thick brush, foraging on strong legs for insects, spiders, berries, and fruit from branches, foliage, and on the ground. The Gray Catbird got its name from its catlike *mew*. Song intersperses *mew* within a variable mixture of melodious, nasal, squeaky, sometimes abrasive but never repeated, notes. Also known to jump abruptly from one phrase to another.

Habitat
Tends to stay hidden in low, dense thickets of under-growth in woodlands and residential areas. Female builds nest in low shrubs or in small trees with dense growth that offers some protection.

Local Sites
The Gray Catbird is common and approachable, but easily overlooked at eye level. Scan the banks of streams in the Pine Barrens for a good look.

FIELD NOTES In addition to the catlike *mew* sound, the Gray Catbird mimics the sounds of other birds, of amphibians, even of machinery, and incorporates them into its song.

Year-round | Adult

NORTHERN MOCKINGBIRD

Mimus polyglottos L 10" (25 cm)

FIELD MARKS
Gray overall; darker above

Blackish wings and tail

White wing patches and outer
tail feathers, which flash
conspicuously in flight

Short, black bill

Behavior
The pugnacious Northern Mockingbird will protect its
territory against not only other birds but also dogs,
cats, and humans. Has a varied diet that includes
berries, grasshoppers, spiders, snails, and earthworms.
A talented mimic, the mockingbird is known for its
variety of song, learning and imitating calls of multiple
species. Typically repeats a song's phrases three times
before beginning a new one. Call is a loud, sharp *check*.

Habitat
Resides in a variety of habitats, including cities, towns
and suburbs. Feeds close to the ground, in thickets or
heavy vegetation.

Local Sites
The Northern Mockingbird is widespread and
abundant throughout New Jersey.

FIELD NOTES If heard only, the Brown Thrasher, *Toxostoma rufum*
(inset), can easily be confused with the mockingbird. Its call is a
sharp *smack* and the varied phrases of its immense repertoire
are always given in two's or three's.
Once spotted, the Brown Thrasher
is readily distinguished by its reddish
brown upperparts and its pale, heavily
streaked underparts.

Nonbreeding | Adult

EUROPEAN STARLING

Sturnus vulgaris L 8½" (22 cm)

FIELD MARKS
Iridescent black breeding plumage

Yellow bill in summer, its base
blue in male, pink in female

Fall feathers tipped in white,
giving speckled appearance

Fall bill darker

Behavior

A social and aggressive bird, the European Starling
feeds on a tremendous variety of food, ranging from
invertebrates—such as snails, worms, and spiders—to
fruits, berries, grains, seeds, and garbage. Its short,
square tail is particularly distinguishable during flight.
Except during nesting season, usually seen in flocks.
Imitates the songs of other species and has high-
pitched call notes that include squeaks, warbles, chirps,
and twittering.

Habitat

The adaptable starling thrives in a variety of habitats,
from urban centers to agricultural regions. Nests
in cavities, ranging from crevices in urban settings to
woodpecker holes and nest boxes.

Local Sites

Widespread year-round throughout New Jersey, the
starling is likely to be found in most local parks.

FIELD NOTES A Eurasian species introduced into New York's
Central Park in 1890 that has since spread throughout the U.S.
and Canada. Abundant, bold, and aggressive, starlings often
compete for and take over nest sites of other birds, including
Eastern Bluebirds, Wood Ducks, Red-bellied Woodpeckers,
Great Crested Flycatchers, and Purple Martins.

Year-round | Adult

CEDAR WAXWING

Bombycilla cedrorum L 7¼" (18 cm)

FIELD MARKS

Distinctive sleek crest

Black mask bordered in white

Brownish breast, sides, head, and back; pale yellow belly; gray rump

Yellow terminal tail band

May have red, waxy tips on wings

Behavior
Eats the most fruit of any bird in North America. Up to 84 percent of diet includes cedar, peppertree, and hawthorn berries and crabapple fruit. Also consumes sap, flower petals, and insects. Cedar Waxwings are gregarious in nature and band together for foraging and protection. Flocks containing several to a few hundred birds may feed side by side in winter, then rapidly disperse, startling potential predators. Call is a thin, high-pitched *zeee*.

Habitat
Found in open habitats where berries are available. The abundance and location of berries influence the Cedar Waxwing's migration patterns: It moves long distances only when its food sources run out.

Local Sites
Waxwings can be found at Higbee's Beach Wildlife Management Area near Cape May, especially during fall migration.

FIELD NOTES Cedar Waxwing mates engage in "courtship hopping." On a shared perch, male and female take turns hopping toward one another until they touch bills. The male passes food to the female. She hops away, returns, and gives it back.

Year-round | Adult male

PROTHONOTARY WARBLER

Protonotaria citrea L 5½" (14 cm)

FIELD MARKS

Male's head and underparts
golden yellow; female duller

Blue-gray wings

Blue-gray tail has white patches;
white undertail coverts

Large dark eyes; long black bill

Behavior

Deliberate in plucking insects, larvae, spiders, and seeds
from crevices in ground, logs, and trees. Also picks
snails and crustaceans right out of water. After arriving
on breeding grounds and building several partial nests,
male sings incessantly until female arrives and chooses
a nest to complete. Song is a series of loud, ringing
zweet notes; call is a dry *chip*.

Habitat

Common in moist lowland forests, woodlands prone to
flooding, and stream banks, but wanders far during
migration. Unlike most warblers, nests in tree cavities,
nest boxes, or similar crannies, always near water.

Local Sites

The cedar swamps of the Pine Barrens provide the
unique habitat this wood-warbler needs to nest,
especially around the old trees of Brendan T. Byrne
State Forest, a section of the Pine Barrens.

FIELD NOTES The Yellow Warbler, *Dendroica petechia*
(inset), shares with the Prothonotary a prominent
dark eye, a bright yellow face, and a preference
for wet habitats, but not forests. The male Yellow
(inset, top), has red streaks on its breast.

Year-round | Adult male

NORTHERN PARULA

Parula americana L 4½" (11 cm)

FIELD MARKS
Gray-blue above with yellowish-green upper back; white belly

Two bold white wing bars

Throat and breast bright yellow

Adult male shows reddish and black breast bands

Behavior
New Jersey's smallest warbler, the Northern Parula is a very active forager and can be observed rightside up or upside down on tree trunks seeking out larvae; hovering in search of caterpillars or spiders, for which its beak is well adapted; or in aerial pursuit of flying insects. Song can be heard from the treetops during nesting or migration, consisting of a rising, buzz-like trill, which ends with an abrupt *zip* in the eastern birds.

Habitat
Common in coniferous or mixed woods, especially near water. Prefers to nest in trees covered with the lichen *Usnea*.

Local Sites
To find a nesting Parula, look for the pale green, stringy *Usnea* lichen hanging from branches of trees in the Delaware Water Gap National Recreation Area. The Parula is a common migrant elsewhere in the state.

FIELD NOTES The Northern Parula is quite picky when it comes to its nesting materials. If it cannot find a tree covered in *Usnea* lichen, it will fly as far as a mile away to secure a single piece for use as padding. A decrease in the amount of this lichen on the Atlantic coast due to air pollution is currently threatening the warbler's population in New Jersey.

Immature | "Myrtle"

YELLOW-RUMPED WARBLER

Dendroica coronata L 5½" (14 cm)

FIELD MARKS
Bright yellow rump; yellow patch
on sides of breast

Yellow on crown while breeding

White wing bars and underparts

Females and fall males duller than
breeding males

Behavior
New Jersey's only regular winter warbler, the Yellow-
rumped is easy to locate and observe darting about
branches from tree to tree, foraging for insects and
spiders in the spring and summer, for myrtle berries
and seeds in winter. Courtship involves intensive
singing. Nest-building and incubation carried out
mainly by the female. Songs of the eastern subspecies,
the "Myrtle Warbler," include a slow warble and a
musical trill.

Habitat
Nests in coniferous or mixed woodlands. Common in
fall and winter in brushy and woodland habitats on
barrier islands, especially in bayberry thickets.

Local Sites
During fall migration, the Yellow-rumped Warbler is
abundant throughout coastal New Jersey, from Sandy
Hook to Cape May. Check the woodland thickets of
Island Beach State Park in October.

FIELD NOTES The eastern subspecies of the Yellow-rumped
Warbler is often referred to as the "Myrtle Warbler," distinguishing it from the western subspecies, "Audubon's Warbler," which
has similar markings, but has a yellow throat rather than a white
one, and lacks the white eyebrow of the Myrtle.

Breeding | Adult male

BLACK-AND-WHITE WARBLER

Mniotilta varia L 5½" (13 cm)

FIELD MARK
Boldly striped black-and-white on
head, body, and undertail coverts

Male's throat and cheeks are
black; in winter, chin is white

Females and immatures have
white cheeks and throats

Behavior
The only warbler that creeps around branches and up
and down tree trunks, foraging like a nuthatch or
creeper; though it does not use its tail to prop up its
body. Probes crevices in the bark of trees with its long
bill for insects, caterpillars, and spiders. If disturbed at
nest, female drags wings on the ground with tail spread
for distraction. Song is a series of high, thin *wee-see*
notes; calls include a sharp *chip* and a high *seep-seep*.

Habitat
Prefers forests, both deciduous and mixed woodlands,
as well as forested margins of swamps and rivers. Nests
on the ground, close to the base of a bush or tree, or in
the hollow of a stump or log.

Local Sites
The Black-and-white Warbler is a common breeder in
the woods of Great Swamp National Wildlife Refuge.
Watch for their nests among the leaf litter.

FIELD NOTES Once referred to as the Black-and-white Creeper
due to its creeper-like feeding behavior, the Black-and-white
returns to northern breeding grounds earlier in the spring than
most warblers who must wait for spring leaves to sprout before
they can load up on the insect food needed during migration.

Year-round | Adult male

PINE WARBLER

Dendroica pinus L 5½" (14 cm)

FIELD MARKS
Yellow throat color extends onto
sides of neck and breast

Male is greenish olive above with
dark streaks on sides of breast

Belly and undertail coverts white

Female is duller overall

Behavior

Forages high up in pine trees, gleaning insects, caterpillars, and spiders from bark, leaves, and pinecones, but will also feed on ground and along lower branches for insects, seeds, grapes, and berries. Will also make aerial dives at flying insects. Though territorially aggressive in breeding season toward other species sharing the same stand of pines, in winter the Pine Warbler may feed in mixed flocks with bluebirds and Yellow-rumped Warblers. A very vocal bird, its song is a musical trill, varying in speed. Call is a slurred *tsup*.

Habitat

Favors open stands of pines, especially while breeding; conceals nest among the needles at branch tips. Winters in pines and mixed woodlands.

Local Sites

The Pine Warbler is common in summer in the Pine Barrens of southeastern New Jersey.

FIELD NOTES The Palm Warbler, *Dendroica palmarum* (inset: eastern, top; western, bottom) is distinguished from the Pine by a yellow eyebrow and undertail coverts, and in spring migration by a chestnut cap. It forages on or near the ground, habitually pumping its tail.

Year-round | Adult male

PRAIRIE WARBLER

Dendroica discolor L 4¾" (12 cm)

FIELD MARKS

Olive above with faint chestnut streaks on back of adult male

Bright yellow below with black streaks on sides

Bright yellow above and below eye

Female and immature duller overall

Behavior

A very active bird, it often pumps its tail while foraging for insects and spiders on bushes, low tree branches, or the ground. Joins mixed flocks on migration and in winter. A frequent recipient of the Brown-headed Cowbird's egg-dropping, the Prairie Warbler is becoming even more vulnerable as its habitat is further fragmented by ongoing development. Sings from exposed perch its distinctive song, a rising series of buzzy *zee* notes. Call is a rich, full *chick*.

Habitat

Open woodlands, especially ones with pines, scrublands, and overgrown fields, but not prairies (it was misnamed when first found). Cup-shaped nest is hidden in trees or bushes.

Local Sites

The Prairie Warbler is partial to dune woodlands and open stands of pine. It is particularly numerous in the Pine Barrens.

FIELD NOTES The Kentucky Warbler, *Oporornis formosus* (inset), is characterized by yellow spectacles separating the black on its crown from the black on its face and neck. It also has entirely yellow underparts and bright olive upperparts. It is found in the moist interior of well-vegetated deciduous forests.

Year-round | Adult male

COMMON YELLOWTHROAT

Geothlypis trichas L 5" (13 cm)

FIELD MARKS
Adult male shows broad, black
mask bordered above by light gray

Female lacks black mask, has
whitish eye ring

Bright yellow throat and breast;
olive-gray upperparts; yellow
undertail coverts

Behavior
This widespread warbler generally remains close to
ground, skulking and hiding in undergrowth. May also
be seen climbing vertically on stems. While foraging,
cocks tail and hops on ground to glean insects, caterpillars, and spiders from foliage, twigs, and reeds. Sometimes feeds while hovering, or gives chase to flying
insects. One version of variable song is a loud, rolling
wichity-wichity-wich. Calls include a raspy *chuck*.

Habitat
Stays low in marshes, shrubby fields, and thickets near
water. A solitary nester atop piles of weed and grass, or
in small shrubs.

Local Sites
The Yellowthroat is common in the summer. Look for
it along the streams of the Pine Barrens, in the wet
thickets of Great Swamp, or among the cedar swamps
of Delaware Water Gap National Recreation Area.

FIELD NOTES The colors of the Common Yellowthroat vary widely,
according to geography. Differences include the amount of
yellow on the underparts, the extent of olive shading on the
upperparts, and the color of the border between mask and
crown, which can vary from stark white to gray.

Year-round | Adult

OVENBIRD

Seiurus aurocapilla L 6" (15 cm)

FIELD MARKS
Russet crown bordered by dark stripes

Olive above, white below with dark streaks

Bold white eye ring

Pinkish bill and legs

Behavior
Typically seen on the ground, this warbler walks rather than hops; tail cocked, wings dropped, and head bobbing. Forages among leaves and twigs for insects, caterpillars, earthworms, snails, seeds, fruit, and berries. The Ovenbird is easier to hear than see, as the song of one male will invariably elicit a response from a neighboring male, producing a domino effect until the woods resonate with their competing melodies. Song is a loud, ascending *teacher-teacher-teacher*. Call is a loud *tsick*.

Habitat
Common in mature deciduous and mixed forests. Nests on the ground in a small depression covered with leaf litter and entered on the side, resembling a tiny dutch oven.

Local Sites
The Ovenbird summers in the Charles H. Rogers Wildlife Refuge near Princeton. The forest of High Point State Park is another annual nesting area.

FIELD NOTES In Jamaica, one of its wintering areas, the Ovenbird is known as "Betsy Kickup," for its habit of shifting leaf litter around on the ground to uncover its prey of insects and other arthropods. This foraging technique is usually more typical of sparrows than of warblers.

Year-round | Adult

LOUISIANA WATERTHRUSH

Seiurus motacilla L 6" (15 cm)

FIELD MARKS

White underparts with dark streaking; salmon-buff flanks

Olive-brown above and on crown

Eyebrow is pale buff in front of eye, whiter and broader behind

White, unstreaked chin and throat

Behavior

The Louisiana Waterthrush bobs its tail sideways, slowly but constantly, as it forages on the ground, walking rather than hopping. Feeds on aquatic and terrestrial insects, mollusks, and small fish along stream banks or in shallows. Sings from an exposed perch or on the ground a clear, musical song which begins with three or four downslurred sew notes, followed by a brief, rapid jumble. Call is a sharp *chink*.

Habitat

Found near mountain streams in dense woodlands, also in wooded floodplains and swamps. Nests under roots or in crevices in riparian areas.

Local Sites

The streams and swamps of Delaware Water Gap National Recreation Area host nesting Louisiana Waterthrushes every summer.

FIELD NOTES The Louisiana Waterthrush and its similarly plumaged cousin, the Northern Waterthrush, *Seiurus noveboracensis* (inset), both forage on the ground in wet habitats for similar prey; however, the Louisiana prefers fast-moving streams and floodplains, while the Northern generally stays near calmer waters of bogs, puddles, and pond edges.

Year-round | Adult male

AMERICAN REDSTART

Setophaga ruticilla L 5¼" (13 cm)

FIELD MARKS
Male is glossy black overall

Bright orange patches on sides, wings, and tail

White belly and undertail coverts

Female gray-olive above; white below with yellow patches

Behavior
Often fans its tail and spreads its wings when perched, then darts suddenly to snare flying insects. Also takes insects, caterpillars, spiders, berries, fruit, and seeds from branches and foliage. Broad, flattened bill, ringed by bristles, is well suited for flycatching as well as gleaning. Sings often, a series of high, thin notes generally followed by a single, wheezy, downslurred note. Call is a sweet, rich *chip*.

Habitat
Common in deciduous and mixed woodlands with thick undergrowth, also in riparian and second-growth woodlands. Nests solitarily in forks of trees or bushes 10 to 20 feet from the ground.

Local Sites
Widespread throughout New Jersey in summer, the American Redstart is evident in migration at Higbee's Beach Wildlife Management Area near Cape May.

FIELD NOTES An immature male resembles a female. By the first spring, he has gained black lores and some black spotting on the breast, and his wing and tail patches are a dull orange-yellow. A year-old male trying to breed in this plumage is at a great disadvantage. It is not until his second fall that he acquires full adult plumage and is attractive to females.

Year-round | Adult male

SUMMER TANAGER

Piranga rubra L 7¾" (20 cm)

FIELD MARKS

Adult male is rosy red overall

Most females have olive green
upperparts, yellow underparts

Some females have overall
reddish wash

Large yellowish bill

Behavior

With the largest range of the North American tanagers,
the Summer Tanager reaches its northernmost breeding limit in southern New Jersey. Snags bees and wasps
in midair, sometimes even raiding their hives. After
catching one, the Summer Tanager brings the bee back
to its perch, then beats it against a branch and wipes
the body along bark to remove the stinger before eat-
ing. In addition, deliberately and methodically picks
insects, caterpillars, and fruit from leaves. Melodic,
warbling song is robin-like. Call is a staccato *ki-ti-tuk.*

Habitat

Common in pine-oak woods of the eastern United
States, cottonwood groves in the west. Female builds
nest far up and out on limbs of trees.

Local Sites

Look high up in the trees of the southern Pine Barrens
and in Bellplain State Forest in Cape May County for
this bird's brilliant red plumage.

FIELD NOTES The Scarlet Tanager, *Piranga olivacea*
(inset), commonly migrates to deciduous forests of
the eastern United States. Like the Summer Tanager, the male has a bright red body, but is set apart by
his black wings and tail. The female Scarlet Tanager is
olive above and yellow below with brownish wings and tail.

Year-round | Adult female

EASTERN TOWHEE

Pipilo erythrophthalmus L 7½" (19 cm)

FIELD MARKS

Male shows black upperparts

Rufous sides; white underparts

Distinct white wing patches

White outer tail feathers

Females similarly patterned, but
black areas replaced by brown

Behavior

Remains low to ground, often scratching it with its feet
together, head held low and tail up. This behavior
exposes seeds and insects such as beetles and caterpillars, on which the Eastern Towhee feeds. Also forages
for grasshoppers, spiders, moths, salamanders, and
fruit. Male fans his wings and tail during courtship,
displaying his contrastive white patches. Known to sing
from an exposed perch, *drink your tea*, sometimes
shortened to *drink tea*; though songs vary with each
bird. Also calls in a clear, slightly upslurred *chwee*.

Habitat

Prefers partial to second-growth woodlands, with
dense shrubs, brushy thickets, and extensive leaf litter.
Also seen in brambly fields, hedgerows, riparian areas,
and forest clearings.

Local Sites

Visible in summer in wooded areas throughout New
Jersey, the Eastern Towhee is one of the most abundant
nesters in the Pine Barrens.

FIELD NOTES The juvenile Easter Towhee has brown cap, wings,
and tail, and is heavily streaked with brown, which is especially
distinct on its buff underparts. Look for it only in summer; the molt
into full adult colors takes place its first fall.

Year-round | Adult

FIELD SPARROW

Spizella pusilla L 5¾" (15 cm)

FIELD MARKS
Gray face with reddish crown

Distinct, whitish eye ring; pink bill

Back streaked, except on gray-brown rump

Breast and sides buff-colored, belly grayish white

Behavior
Remains low to the ground in fields and open brush, foraging for insects, caterpillars, seeds, and spiders. Seen in small family groups after nesting and in larger, mixed-species foraging flocks in winter. Song is a series of clear, flute-like whistles accelerating into a trill; call note is a harsh *chip*. In flight, listen for a clear, descending *tsew*.

Habitat
Found in open, brushy woodlands and fields. Female builds nest on the ground or in a bush low to the ground, often near water.

Local Sites
Both the Field and Chipping Sparrows can be found at the Brigantine Division of Edwin B. Forsythe National Wildlife Refuge. The Field Sparrow, not surprisingly, nests in the old fields there.

FIELD NOTES Populating many of the same open woodlands and fields as the Field Sparrow, the Chipping Sparrow, *Spizella passerina* (inset), is distinguished in breeding season by its bright chestnut crown, white eyebrow, and a black line extending through its eye.

Year-round | Adult

SAVANNAH SPARROW

Passerculus sandwichensis L 5½" (14 cm)

FIELD MARKS

Yellow or whitish eyebrow

Pale median crown stripe

Dark-brown streaked upperparts

Buff to white underparts with brown streaking

Pink legs and feet

Behavior

Forages on the ground for insects, spiders, and sometimes snails in the summer; seeds and berries in the fall and winter. When alarmed, often runs through grasses on the ground instead of flying. If pressed, flies only short distance before dropping back down into grasses. Song begins with two or three *chip* notes, then two buzzy trills. Flight call is a thin *seep*.

Habitat

Common in a variety of open habitats: marshes, farm fields, grasslands, golf courses, and grassy dunes. Nests in ground depressions or self-made scrapes in enclaves sheltered by vines or tall grasses.

Local Sites

The Savannah Sparrow's southern breeding limit is in New Jersey, where the piedmont meets the coastal plain. Look for flocks in fall, winter, and spring.

FIELD NOTES A large, pale subspecies of the Savannah Sparrow, known as the Ipswich Sparrow, *Passerculus sandwichensis princeps* (inset), breeds on Sable Island in Nova Scotia, and winters in dune habitats on east coast beaches. It is a regular winter visitor to the dunes of Sandy Hook, part of Gateway National Recreation Area, and at Barnegat Lighthouse State Park.

Year-round | Adult

SONG SPARROW

Melospiza melodia L 5¾-7½" (16-19 cm)

FIELD MARKS
Streaked brown and gray above

Underparts whitish, with heavy streaking on sides and breast

Rounded tail

Broad, grayish eyebrow

Broad, dark malar stripe

Behavior
Scratches ground with feet to unearth grain, seeds, berries, and insects. Also forages in trees and bushes and on the ground for larvae, fruits, and berries. Female broods young while male defends breeding territory intently, singing from exposed perches and battling with competitors. Perches in the open, belting out its melodious song, three to four short, clear notes followed by a buzzy *tow-wee* and a trill. Distinctive call is a nasal, hollow *chimp*.

Habitat
Common in suburban and rural gardens, weedy fields, and dense streamside thickets and forest edges. Nests on the ground or near it in trees and bushes.

Local Sites
The Song Sparrow is a permanent resident throughout New Jersey. A good time to see it is in late spring, when the male will sing from an exposed perch near its nest.

FIELD NOTES There are over 30 recognized subspecies of Song Sparrow, all of which have adapted to specific environments. Pale races, such as *saltonis,* inhabit arid regions in the Southwest; darker races, such as the eastern *melodia,* inhabit more humid regions; and larger races, such as the Alaskan *maxima,* inhabit oceanic islands.

Nonbreeding | Adult

SWAMP SPARROW

Melospiza georgiana L 5¾" (15 cm)

FIELD MARKS

Gray face with reddish crown on breeding adult

Rufous upperparts with black streaking; rufous wings

Gray breast and whitish belly become buffer overall in winter

Behavior

Secretive and solitary, but will respond to "pishing" by birders. Wades into water to pick food from surface. Also gleans insects and seeds from the ground or low vegetation. Forms small, loose groups in the winter. Male feeds the female while she broods eggs. Song is a slow, even-pitched, musical trill, which fades at the end; it is often used to stake claim to a territory. Call notes include a prolonged *zeee,* and a metallic *chip.*

Habitat

Cup-shaped nest is set in reeds or other dense, tall vegetation in marshes, bogs, wet meadows, and near slow streams. Winters in marshes and brushy fields.

Local Sites

You can find the Swamp Sparrow, often with Song Sparrows, among the reeds near ponds of Cape May Point, the Pine Barrens, Great Swamp National Wildlife Refuge, or Forsythe National Wildlife Refuge.

FIELD NOTES The juvenile plumage of this species, only briefly retained, is buffier, especially on the face, flanks, and breast, and is heavily streaked on the underparts. The next molt, to immature plumage, resembles the winter adult with a gray central crown stripe, and rich buff sides and cheeks.

Year-round | Adult

WHITE-THROATED SPARROW

Zonotrichia albicollis L 6¾" (17 cm)

FIELD MARKS

White throat bordered by gray

Black crown stripes and eye line

Broad eyebrow is yellow in front of eye, white or tan behind

Rusty brown above, grayish below; immature duller patterned

Behavior

Employs the double-scratch foraging method of towhees; that is, it rakes leaf litter with a backward kick of both feet, keeping its head held low and its tail pointed up. Also forages in bushes and trees for seeds, fruit, tree buds, and insects. Often heard before seen, its calls include a sharp *pink* and a drawn out, lisping *tseep*. Its song, sung year-round, is a slow, thin whistle consisting of two single notes then three triple notes: *oh-sweet-Canada-Canada-Canada.*

Habitat

Common in woodland undergrowth, brush, and gardens; frequently seen at platform feeders. Nests on the ground or close to it, often at forest edges.

Local Sites

Listen for winter flocks raking leaf litter along forest edges and at feeders. This bird responds well to "pishing" by birders.

FIELD NOTES A migrant and winter visitor to New Jersey, the adult White-crowned Sparrow, *Zonotrichia leucophrys* (inset), is characterized by a black-and-white striped crown and grayish underparts. Immatures have rusty brown and pale crown stripes. This bird can often be seen during fall migration passing through Cape May.

Year-round | Adult male "Slate-colored"

DARK-EYED JUNCO

Junco hyemalis L 6¼" (16 cm)

FIELD MARKS
Variable dark upperparts; whitish underparts

Gray or brown head and breast, sharply set off in most races

White outer tail feathers in flight

Juveniles of all races are streaked

Behavior
Scratches on ground and forages by gleaning seeds, grain, berries, insects, caterpillars, and fruit from plants. Will occasionally give chase to a flying insect. Male gathers material for nest, which female builds. Forms flocks in winter, when males may remain farther north or at greater elevations than juveniles and females. Song is a musical trill that varies in pitch and tempo. Calls include a sharp *dit,* and a rapid twittering in flight.

Habitat
Breeds in coniferous or mixed woodlands, and in bogs. Winters in a wide variety of habitats throughout much of North America. Nests on or close to ground, either sheltered by a bush, or in a cavity such as a tree root.

Local Sites
The "Slate-colored" race, slate-gray above, white below, is abundant and conspicuous in winter in wooded areas and at feeders across New Jersey. You may find a streaked juvenile in summer in High Point State Park.

FIELD NOTES The different subspecies of the Dark-eyed Junco were unified under the same species heading by the American Ornithologists' Union in 1973, although they are widely scattered geographically and fairly disparate in their field marks. They all have in common white outer tail feathers, behavioral habits, and, most significantly, genetic makeup.

Year-round | Adult male

NORTHERN CARDINAL

Cardinalis cardinalis L 8¾" (22 cm)

FIELD MARKS
Male is red overall, with black face

Female is buffy brown tinged with red on wings, crest, and tail

Conspicuous crest

Cone-shaped, reddish bill

Behavior
Forages on the ground or low in shrubs mainly for seeds, leaf buds, berries, and fruit. A nonmigratory songbird, the Cardinal has adapted so well to landscaped yards and backyard feeders that it continues to expand its range northward into Canada. Aggressive in defending its territory, a Cardinal will attack not only other birds, but also itself, reflected in windows, rearview mirrors, chrome surfaces, and hubcaps. Sings a variety of melodious songs year-round, including a *cue cue-cue*, a *cheer-cheer-cheer,* and a *purty-purty-purty.*

Habitat
Year-round resident in gardens and parks, woodland edges, streamside thickets, and practically any environment that provides thick, brushy cover. Nests in forks of trees and bushes, or in tangles of twigs and vines.

Local Sites
Listen for the Cardinals' courtship duets in spring and summer almost anywhere in the state.

FIELD NOTES Another member of the family *Cardinalidae,* the Rose-breasted Grosbeak, *Pheucticus ludovicianus,* breeds in northern New Jersey every summer. The breeding male (inset) has a black head and back, a triangular patch of red on its breast, red wing linings, and white underparts.

Breeding | Adult male

INDIGO BUNTING

Passerina cyanea L 5½" (14 cm)

FIELD MARKS
Breeding male's plumage is deep
blue overall

Winter male's blue is obscured by
brown and buff edges

Female is brownish, with diffuse
streaking on breast and flanks

Behavior
In spring and summer, forages for insects from ground
level to canopy, switching to a mainly seed and berry
diet in the fall and winter. Uses its heavy conical bill to
crack or hull seeds. Sings in a series of varied phrases,
usually doubled, *sweet-sweet* or *here-here*, often ending
with a trill. Second-year males appear to learn songs
from competing males, rather than from parents.

Habitat
Prefers edges and bushy transition zones between old
fields and woodlands. Range is the greatest of all
buntings, extending northward to southern Canada.
Nests in dense shrubs and low trees.

Local Sites
Indigo Buntings summer in the forest edges and fields
of Hutcheson Memorial Forest, a natural research area
in Somerset County run by Rutgers University. Also try
Higbee Beach Wildlife Management Area in Cape May.

FIELD NOTES The Blue Grosbeak, *Passerina caerulea* (inset), a
summer resident in southern New Jersey, is larger
than the Indigo Bunting, and has a heavier bill. The
breeding male (inset, right) is mostly blue with a
black face and chestnut wing bars. The female
and juvenile (inset, center and left) resemble
the Indigo Bunting, except for chestnut wing
bars, bill shape, and overall size.

Breeding | Adult

Sturnella magna L 9½" (24 cm)

FIELD MARKS
Yellow below, with black V-shaped
breast band

Black-and-white striped crown,
with yellow supraloral area

Brown above streaked with black

White outer tail feathers in flight

Behavior
Jerky flight, during which its call is a buzzy *drzzt*. Flicks
its tail open and shut while foraging on the ground,
feeding mainly on insects during spring and summer,
seeds and agricultural grain in late fall and winter.
Generally solitary in summer, the Meadowlark forms
small flocks in fall and winter. Male known to brood
while female starts second nest. Often perches on fence
posts or telephone poles to sing a clear, whistled *see-you
see-yeeer*.

Habitat
In New Jersey, prefers the open space offered by
pastures, meadows, and farm fields. Constructs a
domed nest on the ground that is often woven into
the surrounding live grasses.

Local Sites
Listen for the rich, musical, territorial song of the
Eastern Meadowlark, carrying across the open fields of
Great Swamp National Wildlife Refuge in summer.

FIELD NOTES Though its breeding range has been advancing
northward due to widespread clearing of forests, the Eastern
Meadowlark population has been slowly declining in the eastern
states during the past few decades as it loses suitable habitat to
suburban sprawl.

Year-round | Adult male

RED-WINGED BLACKBIRD

Agelaius phoeniceus L 8¾" (22 cm)

FIELD MARKS

Male is glossy black

Bright red shoulder patches broadly edged with buffy yellow

Wings slightly rounded at tips

Females are dark brown above, heavily streaked below

Behavior

The male's bright red shoulder patches are usually visible when it sings from a perch, often atop a cattail or tall weed stalk, defending its territory. At other times only the yellow border may be visible. Territorially aggressive, a male's social status is dependent on the amount of red he displays on his shoulders. Runs and hops while foraging for insects, seeds, and grains in pastures and open fields. Known to damage crops in farms of southern New Jersey. Song is a liquid, gurgling *konk-la-reee,* ending in a trill. Call is a *chack* note.

Habitat

Breeds in colonies, mainly in freshwater marshes and wet fields with thick vegetation. Nests in cattails, bushes, or dense grass near water. During winter, flocks forage in wooded swamps and farm fields.

Local Sites

The Red-winged is common year-round throughout New Jersey.

FIELD NOTES The number of Red-winged Blackbirds in New Jersey increases exponentially when large flocks arrive from the north in late fall. Very often the majority of blackbirds in large winter flocks are Red-wingeds.

Year-round | Adult male

COMMON GRACKLE

Quiscalus quiscula L 12½" (32 cm)

FIELD MARKS
Plumage appears all black; in good light, males show glossy purplish blue head, neck, breast

Long, wedge-shaped tail

Pale yellow eyes

Pointed beak

Behavior
Rarely seen outside of a flock in winter, this grackle moves to large, noisy, communal roosts in the evening. During the day, mainly seen on the ground in a group, feeding on insects, spiders, grubs, and earthworms. Also wades into shallow water to forage for minnows and crayfish. Known to feast on eggs and baby birds. Courtship display consists of male puffing out shoulder feathers to make a collar, drooping his wings, and singing. These birds produce sounds like ripping cloth or cracking twigs. Call note is a loud *chuck*.

Habitat
Prefers open spaces provided by farm fields, pastures, marshes, and suburban yards; requires wooded areas, especially conifers, for nesting and roosting.

Local Sites
Common Grackles are abundant and gregarious throughout New Jersey. Look for their courtship displays in March or April at Great Swamp.

FIELD NOTES The closely related Boat-tailed Grackle, *Quiscalus major* (inset), a resident of coastal saltmarshes, is larger than the Common Grackle and has duller, brownish eyes. Look for its long, keel-shaped tail at Forsythe National Wildlife Refuge.

BLACKBIRDS, GRACKLES, ORIOLES

Year-round | Adult male

BROWN-HEADED COWBIRD

Molothrus ater L 7½" (19 cm)

FIELD MARKS

Male's brown head contrasts with metallic green-black body

Female gray-brown above, paler below with a dusky malar stripe

Short, dark, pointed bill

Juveniles streaked below

Behavior

Often forages on the ground among herds of cattle, feeding on insects flushed by the grazing farm animals. Also feeds heavily on grass seeds and agricultural grain, and is sometimes viewed as a threat to crops. Generally cocks its tail up while feeding. Most species of cowbird are nest parasites and lay their eggs in the nests of other species, leaving the responsibilities of feeding and fledging of young to the host birds. Song is a squeaky, gurgling call that includes a squeaky whistle.

Habitat

Cowbirds prefer open habitat such as farmlands, pastures, prairies, and edgelands bordering forests. Also found in general around human habitation.

Local Sites

Brown-headed Cowbirds utilize the nests of a variety of birds in the woods of Great Swamp National Wildlife Refuge and Charles H. Rogers Wildlife Refuge.

FIELD NOTES The Brown-headed Cowbird flourishes throughout North America, adapting to newly cleared lands and exposing new songbirds—now more than 200 species—to its parasitic brooding habit. The female Brown-headed Cowbird lays up to 40 eggs a season in the nests of host birds, frequently destroying host eggs in the process.

Breeding | Adult male

BALTIMORE ORIOLE

Icterus galbula L 8¼" (22 cm)

FIELD MARKS

Male has black hood and back, bright orange rump and under-parts, large orange patches on tail

Female is olive-brown above, orange below, with variable black on head and throat

Black wings with white edging

Behavior

Named for the orange-and-black family coat of arms of Lord Baltimore, this widespread migrant prefers caterpillars, but will feed as well on other insects, berries, fruits, even flower nectar. Forages quite high up in bushes and trees. Male bows to female, with wings and tail spread, during courtship. Common calls are a rich *hew-li* and a series of rattling notes. Song is a musical, irregular sequence of whistled *hew li*s.

Habitat

Common breeder in deciduous woodlands of the eastern United States. Also found around human habitation. Suspends its bag-shaped nest near the tip of a tree branch, usually about 30 feet up, an adaptation designed to deter egg-eating snakes and mammals.

Local Sites

Look for this striking bird by itself or in a small family group at Great Swamp National Wildlife Refuge before July, when they begin their southward migration.

FIELD NOTES Sharing much of the same breeding and wintering grounds as the Baltimore Oriole, the Orchard Oriole, *Icterus spurius,* spends most of its time in open woodlands, farmlands, and orchards. The male (inset, bottom) has a black hood and chestnut underparts. The female (inset, top) is olive above and yellow below with dusky wings.

Year-round | Adult male

HOUSE FINCH

Carpodacus mexicanus L 6" (15 cm)

FIELD MARKS
Male's front of head, bib, and rump typically red, but can be orange or, occasionally, yellow

Brown upperparts

Bib set off from streaked underparts

Female streaked brown overall

Behavior
A seed eater, the House Finch forages on the ground, in fields, and in suburban yards. An acrobatic forager, it will also hang upside down to reach seeds or buds. Often visits backyard feeders. Has somewhat undulating flight, and a squared-off tail. Males sing a conspicuously lively, high-pitched song consisting of varied three-note phrases, usually ending in a nasal *wheer*. Calls include a whistled *wheat*.

Habitat
Adaptable to varied habitats, this abundant bird prefers open areas in the East, including suburban parks and areas where it can nest on buildings.

Local Sites
The House Finch is widespread and abundant year-round throughout New Jersey.

FIELD NOTES The Purple Finch, *Carpodacus purpureus,* is not purple but rose-red on the body of the adult male (inset, bottom). The female (inset, top) is gray-brown above and heavily streaked below, with a bolder face pattern and a more deeply notched tail than the House Finch. The Purple Finch is an uncommon migrant and winter visitor.

Breeding | Adult male

AMERICAN GOLDFINCH

Carduelis tristis L 5" (13 cm)

FIELD MARKS
Breeding male bright yellow with
black cap; female and winter male
duller overall, lacking cap

Black wings have white bars

Black-and-white tail; white uppertail and undertail coverts

Behavior
The state bird of New Jersey, the American Goldfinch is
gregarious and active. Winter flocks may contain a
hundred or more goldfinches and include several other
species. The typical finch diet, mostly seeds, is the most
vegetarian of any North American bird; the American
Goldfinch, however, will sometimes eat insects as well.
During courtship, the male performs exaggerated,
undulating aerial maneuvers, and often feeds the incu-
bating female. Song is a lively series of trills, twitters,
and *swee* notes. Distinctive flight call is *per-chik-o-ree*.

Habitat
Found in weedy fields, open second-growth woodlands, and on roadsides, especially territory rich in
thistles and sunflowers, or at special goldfinch feeders.
Often nests at edges of open areas or in old fields.

Local Sites
The American Goldfinch nests quite late into the
season in clearings within the Pine Barrens, or in parks
and open areas throughout the state.

FIELD NOTES Sometimes a cowbird will lay its eggs in the nest
of an American Goldfinch. Although the eggs will hatch, most
young cowbirds die before they leave the nest, due to their
inability to obtain enough protein from the finch's seed diet.

Breeding | Adult male

HOUSE SPARROW

Passer domesticus L 6¼" (16 cm)

FIELD MARKS
Breeding male has black bill, bib, and lores; gray crown; chestnut nape, back, and shoulders

Female has brown back, streaked with black; buffy eyestripe; and unstreaked grayish breast

Behavior
Abundant and gregarious year-round. Feeds on grains, seeds, and shoots, or seeks out bird feeders for sunflower seeds and millet. Also forages on the ground, getting food from plants or animal dung. In urban areas, House Sparrows may beg for food from humans and will clean up any crumbs left behind. Females choose mates mostly according to song display. Singing males give persistent *cheep*.

Habitat
Found in close proximity to humans. Can be observed in urban and suburban areas and in rural landscapes inhabited by humans and livestock.

Local Sites
Abundant wherever humans habitate, House Sparrows flock in the most heavily urbanized areas.

FIELD NOTES Also known as the English Sparrow, the House Sparrow was first introduced into North America in New York's Central Park around 1850, in an effort to populate the park with all the birds mentioned in Shakespeare's plays. It has since spread across the continent to become one of the most successful bird species in North America. Ironically, its numbers are declining precipitously in its native England.

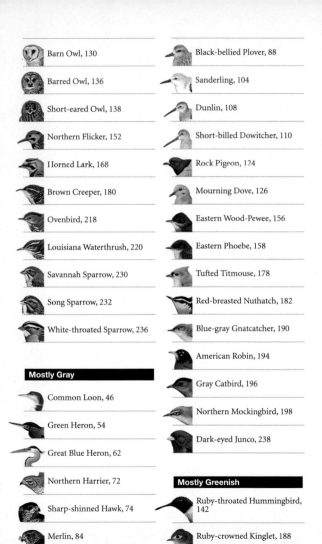

Mostly Orange and Black

 American Redstart, 222

 Baltimore Oriole, 252

Mostly Red

 Summer Tanager, 224

 Northern Cardinal, 240

 House Finch, 254

Mostly White

 Snow Goose, 12

 Tundra Swan, 18

 Snowy Egret, 58

 Great Egret, 60

 Ring-billed Gull, 114

 Royal Tern, 118

 Forster's Tern, 120

Mostly Yellow

 White-eyed Vireo, 162

 Prothonotary Warbler, 204

 Pine Warbler, 212

 Prairie Warbler, 214

 Common Yellowthroat, 216

 Eastern Meadowlark, 244

 American Goldfinch, 256

Prominent Green Head

 Wood Duck, 20

 Mallard, 22

 Common Merganser, 36

The main entry for each species is listed in **boldface** type and refers to the text page opposite the illustration.

A check-off box is provided next to each common-name entry so that you can use this index as a checklist of the species you have identified.

ACKNOWLEDGMENTS

The Book Division would like to thank the following people for their guidance and contribution in creating the *National Geographic Field Guide to Birds: New Jersey*

Tom Vezo:
Tom Vezo is an award-winning wildlife photographer who is widely published throughout the U.S. and Europe. Located out of Green Valley, Arizona, he specializes in bird photography but photographs other wildlife and nature subjects as well. He is also a contributor to the *National Geographic Reference Atlas to the Birds of North America.* For a look at more of his images, find his gallery at tomvezo.com.

Brian E. Small:
Brian E. Small has been a full-time professional wildlife photographer specializing in birds for more than 15 years. In addition, he has been a regular columnist and Advisory Board member for *WildBird* magazine for the past 10 years. An avid naturalist and enthusiastic birder, Brian is currently the Photo Editor for the American Birding Association's *Birding* magazine. You can find more of his images at www.briansmallphoto.com.

Cortez C. Austin, Jr.:
Cortez Austin is a wildlife photographer who specializes in North American and tropical birds. He has a degree in zoology and has done graduate work in conservation, ecology, and microbiology. An ardent conservationist, he has donated images, given lectures, and written book reviews for conservation organizations. In addition he has published numerous articles and photographs in birding magazines in the United States. His photographs have also appeared in field guides, books, and brochures on wildlife.

Bates Littlehales:
National Geographic photographer for more than 30 years covering myriad subjects around the globe, Bates Littlehales continues to specialize in photographing birds and is an expert in capturing their beauty and ephemeral nature. Bates is co-author of the *National Geographic Photographic Field Guide: Birds,* and a contributor to the *National Geographic Reference Atlas to the Birds of North America.*

Rulon Simmons:
Co-author of the *National Geographic Photographic Field Guide: Birds,* Rulon Simmons worked 32 years for the Eastman Kodak Company, until his division moved to ITT Industries. Rulon's work at ITT's Space Systems Division involves optimizing image quality of aircraft and satellite imaging. Combining his skill in photography with his passion for birding, he photographs species across North America.

Cover Tom Vezo; 2 Bates Littlehales; 12 Tom Vezo; 14 Tom Vezo;
16 Cortez C. Austin Jr.; 18 Tom Vezo; 20 Cortez C. Austin Jr.; 22 Bates
Littlehales; 24 Tom Vezo; 26 Tom Vezo; 28 Brian E. Small; 30 Tom Vezo;
32 Rulon Simmons; 34 Tom Vezo; 36 Cortez C. Austin Jr.; 38 Brian E.
Small; 40 Rulon Simmons; 42 Tom Vezo; 44 Tom Vezo; 46 Tom Vezo;
48 Tom Vezo; 50 Cortez C. Austin Jr.; 52 Tom Vezo; 54 Tom Vezo; 56 Tom
Vezo; 58 Tom Vezo; 60 Cortez C. Austin Jr.; 62 Tom Vezo; 64 Tom Vezo;
66 Tom Vezo; 68 Rulon Simmons; 70 Brian E. Small; 72 Ron Austing, Frank
Lane Picture Agency/CORBIS; 74 Tom Vezo; 76 Tom Vezo; 78 Tom Vezo;
80 Tom Vezo; 82 Tom Vezo; 84 Tom Vezo; 86 Tom Vezo; 88 Tom Vezo;
90 Brian E. Small; 92 Cortez C. Austin Jr.; 94 Tom Vezo; 96 Tom Vezo;
98 Tom Vezo; 100 Brian E. Small; 102 Tom Vezo; 104 Brian E. Small;
106 Brian E. Small; 108 Brian E. Small; 110 Cortez C. Austin Jr.; 112 Cortez
C. Austin Jr.; 114 Tom Vezo; 116 Tom Vezo; 118 Brian E. Small; 120 Cortez
C. Austin Jr.; 122 Cortez C. Austin Jr.; 124 Tom Vezo; 126 Tom Vezo;
128 Brian E. Small; 130 Tom Vezo; 132 Tom Vezo; 134 Bates Littlehales;
136 Tom Vezo; 138 Tom Vezo; 140 Lynda Richardson/CORBIS; 142 Bates
Littlehales; 144 Brian E. Small; 146 Tom Vezo; 148 Tom Vezo; 150 Bates
Littlehales; 152 Tom Vezo; 154 Tom Vezo; 156 Brian E. Small; 158 Tom
Vezo; 160 Tom Vezo; 162 Brian E. Small; 164 Tom Vezo; 166 Tom Vezo;
168 Brian E. Small; 170 Tom Vezo; 172 Tom Vezo; 174 Cortez C. Austin Jr.;
176 Bates Littlehales; 178 Tom Vezo; 180 Brian E. Small; 182 Tom Vezo;
184 Brian E. Small; 186 Tom Vezo; 188 Tom Vezo; 190 Tom Vezo; 192 Brian
E. Small; 194 Bates Littlehales; 196 Tom Vezo; 198 Brian E. Small; 200 Brian
E. Small; 202 Cortez C. Austin Jr.; 204 Brian E. Small; 206 Tom Vezo;
208 Tom Vezo; 210 Brian E. Small; 212 Brian E. Small; 214 Tom Vezo;
216 Bates Littlehales; 218 Tom Vezo; 220 Brian E. Small; 222 Bates
Littlehales; 224 Brian E. Small; 226 Bates Littlehales; 228 Brian E. Small;
230 Bates Littlehales; 232 Tom Vezo; 234 Tom Vezo; 236 Brian E. Small;
238 Tom Vezo; 240 Cortez C. Austin Jr.; 242 Brian E. Small; 244 Cortez C.
Austin Jr.; 246 Tom Vezo; 248 Tom Vezo; 250 Tom Vezo; 252 Tom Vezo;
254 Tom Vezo; 256 Brian E. Small; 258 Tom Vezo

FIELD NOTES

NATIONAL GEOGRAPHIC
FIELD GUIDE TO BIRDS:
NEW JERSEY

Edited by Jonathan Alderfer

**Published by
the National Geographic Society**

John M. Fahey, Jr.,
President and Chief Executive Officer

Gilbert M. Grosvenor,
Chairman of the Board

Nina D. Hoffman,
Executive Vice President

Prepared by the Book Division

Kevin Mulroy,
Senior Vice President and Publisher

Kristin Hanneman, *Illustrations Director*

Marianne R. Koszorus, *Design Director*

Carl Mehler, *Director of Maps*

Barbara Brownell Grogan,
Executive Editor

Staff for this Book

Jonathan Alderfer, *Editor*

Dan O'Toole, *Writer, Project Manager*

Megan McCarthy, *Designer*

Carol Norton, *Series Art Director*

Kristin Hanneman, Dan O'Toole,
Illustrations Editors

Rachel Sweeney, *Illustrations Assistant*

Suzanne Poole, *Text Editor*

Matt Chwastyk,
Map Production

Rick Wain, *Production Project Manager*

Manufacturing and Quality Control

Christopher A. Liedel,
Chief Financial Officer

Phillip L. Schlosser, *Managing Director*

John T. Dunn, *Technical Director*

One of the world's largest nonprofit scientific and educational organizations, the National Geographic Society was founded in 1888 "for the increase and diffusion of geographic knowledge." Fulfilling this mission, the Society educates and inspires millions every day through its magazines, books, television programs, videos, maps and atlases, research grants, the National Geographic Bee, teacher workshops, and innovative classroom materials. The Society is supported through membership dues, charitable gifts, and income from the sale of its educational products. This support is vital to National Geographic's mission to increase global understanding and promote conservation of our planet through exploration, research, and education.

For more information, please call
1-800-NGS LINE (647-5463) or write
to the following address:

National Geographic Society
1145 17th Street N.W.
Washington, D.C. 20036-4688 U.S.A.

Visit the Society's Web site at
www.nationalgeographic.com.

**Library of Congress
Cataloging-in-Publication Data**

Available upon request.